A FULTON SHEEN READER

Carillon Books

A Fulton Sheen Reader
A Carillon Book

Carillon Books Edition published 1979

ISBN 0-89310-037-4 (hardbound)
         0-89310-038-2 (paperbound)

Library of Congress Catalog Card Number 78-575-96

Carillon Books is a division of
CATHOLIC DIGEST
2115 Summit Ave.
St. Paul, Minnesota 55105
U.S.A.

Foreword

The editors at *Carillon Books* decided to call the present volume *A Fulton Sheen Reader* rather than *The Fulton Sheen Reader*. The title chosen implies properly that in a very real sense any selection of a given length from the Archbishop's works would be as excellent as any other selection. To use the word *the* in the title would imply that there was a body of work the reader could afford to pass over. So while we believe the chapters here are equal to anything he ever wrote we do not assert their superiority to all others.

But our selection was not made at random. Due weight was given to fields for which the writing was done: television, newspaper columns and books. Books, or course, included historical, devotional, sociological and apologetical titles.

Consideration was given to the times periods during which Archbishop Sheen wrote. The clever reader will be able to date some of the selections by references to then-present things like Fascism and Nazism, but if he is all that clever he will see that the arguments presented by the author for the Catholic side can be used with equal force against evils prevalent in our own 1970's. As Fulton Sheen certainly remarked somewhere or other, error changes but truth does not.

Any reader, Catholic or not, "interested" in God and religion would do well to read all of the Archbishop's work, failing that, he can get a sighting on the full spectrum of Sheen's achievement in this book.

Contents

† 1 †

My Four Writers

The most honest of those who appear on radio or television, as regards their material, are the comedians. At the end of every program, regardless of who the comedian is, there will always be found listed the names of his writers. The comedians admit, though they speak the humorous lines, that they actually are indebted to others for putting them in their mouths. One never sees on a television screen at the end of a program given by a politician the name of the one who wrote his speech. It is even common today for those who sign their names to books never to give any credit to their ghost writers who did all the writing. Robert Benchley once said, "It took me fifteen years to discover that I had no talent for writing, but I couldn't give it up because by that time I was too famous."

Here we pay tribute to the four writers who have given us the greatest inspiration:

1. A collector of internal revenue
2. A reporter
3. A physician
4. An official in a fishing company

These four writers are perhaps better known as Matthew, Mark, Luke, and John. Though none of them has written the material that is used in our books, they nevertheless have given us the philosophy and theology behind all that we write. Outside of these, we have no writers.

The *dates* at which each wrote are as follows:

Matthew wrote a Gospel in Aramaic about the year 42 A.D., translated into Greek about the year 55.

Mark wrote his Gospel between the years 53 and 63.

Luke wrote between 60 and 63.

John wrote about the year 100.

The *audiences* for which they wrote were different, which accounts for the variations of each Gospel. These differences would already be explicable by the fact that each receives the treasure of the spirit in an earthly vessel. Since the enlightenment of each is according to his individuality and his capacity to receive truth, as well as the power to express it, there would be variations. Light is the same by nature and is governed by fixed laws, but its reflections are infinitely varied, depending upon the surfaces upon which it plays. Since the four Evangelists directed their Gospels to somewhat different audiences, there are varying emphasis and diverse appeals, though all concern the same basic idea of presenting the story of Christ the Son of the Living God.

Matthew addressed his Gospel to the Jews; Mark, to the Romans; Luke, principally to the Greeks; John, to all Christians.

Matthew. Matthew was a publican—a tax collector or customs officer in the territory of Herod Antipas. He collected the taxes for the Romans in somewhat the same way that a Pole might collect taxes for Soviet Russia in contemporary Poland. In addition, therefore, to being a tax collector, he was in modern language a Quisling, in the sense that he was disloyal to his own people for having sold himself out to the conquerors. His tax office was at Capharnaum, on the great west road from Damascus to the Mediterranean. One day while he was seated at his counting table, Our Blessed Lord summoned him to be an Apostle. A short time afterward he entertained Our Lord at a feast to which he invited tax gatherers and other persons who were regarded as sinners. It was interesting that the banquet should have been made up for the most part of those who, possibly like Matthew, came from the Roman office of internal revenue.

His background accounts for the frequent use of money in his Gospel. Mark refers to three coins and only the poorest; Luke refers to the mite and the farthing and even the pound, but Matthew, who was in the habit of handling money, refers to coins of the highest value; for example, the talent. He uses three words which occur nowhere else in the Gospels; "tribune," "piece of money," and "talent." He also uses gold, silver, and brass, which do not occur in Mark, Luke, or John.

Writing as Matthew did for the Jews, he puts forth Our Lord in His regal aspect of the Messias in fulfillment of the prophecies to the Old Testament. The genealogy is traced from Abraham, the father of the Jewish people. Every possible incident in the life of Our Lord is presented as the predestined accomplishment of the predictions of the Old Testament. There are 129 Old Testament references, citations, and allusions. The one argument that might convince the Jews of the continuity of the Old and New Testament was the fulfillment of prophecies. He applies the Old Testament to the outstanding events in Our Lord's life, such as the Virgin Birth, the Birth in Bethlehem, the return from Egypt, the preaching in Galilee, miracles, parables, triumphant entrance into Jerusalem, and the price of Judas's treason. Turning over the pages of the Old Testament, citing Isaias, Jeremias, Micheas, David, Machabees, he who had been a traitor and disloyal to his people now begins to discover the glory of his race and the nobility of its traditions, as he proclaims that Christ is the Son of the Living God, the Expected of the nations, the Messias of the Jewish people. He who had been disloyal now becomes one of the greatest patriots and lovers of the tradition of the Old Testament because he had found his God.

Luke. Luke was a physician and is called by St. Paul "the most dear physician." Born in Antioch, Luke belonged by birth and education to the Greek world. Quite apart from the fact that contemporary evidence states that he was a physician, it is rather evident from his use of medical terms. He shows a preference for stories of healing; his language is colored by technical medical terms. He modifies Mark's caustic comment: "And now a woman who for twelve years had had an issue of blood, and had undergone much from many physicians, spending all she had on them, and no better for it but rather grown worse, came up behind Jesus in the crowd. . . ." Luke softens this in his Gospel to read: "And a woman who for twelve years had had an issue of blood, and spent all her money on doctors without finding one who could cure her. . . ." Luke implies that her case was chronic, and thus the physicians could not be blamed for not having cured her, thereby defending the integrity of his profession.

In describing a demoniac, Luke notes that the evil spirit came out of him without having done him any harm. He describes the cure of Peter's mother-in-law as if in careful contemplation of the symptoms of the patient. He speaks of two distinct kinds of leprosy, and with a doctor's precision notes that it was the right hand of the certain man that was withered, and the right ear of Malchus that was lost. Luke does not use the ordinary word for needle, which is *rhaphis* and which is used by Mark and Matthew, but says, *"dia trematos belones"* (*belone* was a surgical needle—a word used by Galen, a Greek physician who lived 130 to 200 A.D.). Luke quotes Isaias referring to Our Lord's healing mission and of the six miracles peculiar to Luke, five are miracles of healing. In the story of the Good Samaritan, he uses such expressions as "half dead," "bound up his wounds," "pouring on them oil and wine," indicating a professional interest. Luke records that Our Lord sent forth his missionaries both to preach and to heal; he also preserves Our Lord's proverb: "Physician, heal thyself."

His Gospel was addressed to the Gentiles in general and to the Greeks in particular. That is why Jewish customs and localities are explained. For example, he says that Capharnaum is a city of Galilee, and that the feast of the unleavened bread is called the Passover, and he gives the distance of Emmaus from Jerusalem, which would be familiar only to those living in Palestine.

Inasmuch as Luke was writing for the Gentiles in general and the Greeks in particular, we find the one note struck through-out the Gospel which would appeal to the Greeks, namely, the note of universalism. When Alexander had defeated the Persians, he said that "God is the Father of all men." In Luke there is no narrow nationalism, but a broad outlook on the world. Men are seen as men of whatever nation or clime, and Our Lord is presented as the Redeemer of them all. It was only natural that, being a Gentile, that Divine thoughtfulness for all humanity should take hold of him. His pen, though a reed shaken with Divine inspiration, moved in the direction of human sympathies; he let humanity absorb nationality. Hence though Matthew traces the genealogy of Our Lord back to Abraham, Luke goes back to the fountainhead where all divergent streams meet, namely, to Adam, in order the better to describe the new Adam, Christ. He tells of "good tidings to all people." He records the first discourse at Nazareth, showing how in ancient times even the mercy of God flowed out to the Gentile widow and a Gentile leper. He alone mentions the mission of the seventy whose number was a prophecy of the worldwide gospel, seventy being the recognized symbol of the Gentile world. Luke alone gives the story of the Good Samaritan, showing that the virtue of compassion dwelt in humanity. He tells the story of Zacchaeus, the Gentile publican, and how Our Lord passed him along to the inheritance of Abraham. He gives the Parables of the Lost Coin, the Prodigal Son, and the Lost Sheep in order to show how Our Blessed Lord came "to save that which was lost," namely, humanity. To emphasize further the note of universality, he above all the Evangelists writes about women. The word "woman" occurs in Matthew thirty times; in Mark nineteen; in John, nineteen, but in Luke, forty-three. His Gospel records the word "sinner" more than all of the other Gospels together. Matthew mentions "sinner" five times; Mark, five times; John, four, but Luke, sixteen. What is particularly interesting is that Luke, a physician, and therefore skilled in obstetrics, is the one who, from a natural point of view, might be presumed to be the last to be convinced of the Virgin Birth, yet he is the one who records it.

Mark. Mark was the son of a wealthy woman who lived near Jerusalem and whose home was the meeting place of many of the early Christians. That Mark was a reporter is rather evident from an incident that happened in the closing hours of Our Blessed Lord's earthly life. The night Our Saviour was betrayed and all who were with Him fled, there was one who followed, though he was not with Him in the Garden. As the soldiers came out on the public road, an obscure young man did what others feared to do—took a few steps in the company of Our Lord. When the soldiers laid hold of him and pulled the garment from his body, he fled naked into the night. Whether Mark's interest for having spot news began that particular night we do not know, but it is very clear that he was a follower of Peter, and from Peter derived most of the information in his Gospel. Mark was with Peter in the year 64 A.D. when Peter wrote his first letter from the Imperial capital. Peter calls Mark his "son." Furthermore, the Gospel points to an eyewitness as its author, either directly or indirectly. The many details mentioned in the Gospel of Mark are such that they could come only from a careful eyewitness such as Peter. Being a fisherman, he was used to watching the least sign of the presence of fish and thereby became a keen observer. From his trade he preserved a special aptitude for noticing and remembering the contour of a picture. All of these details Peter gave to Mark, such as that of a man sick with palsy being carried on his pallet by four men. Mark notes that men sat down in ranks of 150 "upon the green grass." Mark also mentions six distinct looks of Our Lord and indicates the gestures as well as the emotions of the Saviour.

Because of this close relation of Mark to Peter, almost everything unfavorable is reported about Peter, and nothing favorable. For example, the severe rebuke to Peter is recorded, although there is no mention of the noble confession of the Divinity of Christ which Peter had just made. Mark is the one who singles out Peter as the one whom Our Lord addressed when His three Apostles slept in the Garden: "Simon, sleepest thou?" Mark also gives the details of Peter's denial of Our Lord to the maidservant.

Mark is the one who records the cure of Peter's mother-in-law; therefore, Peter must not have been ungrateful to the Good Lord for the cure of the woman.

Inasmuch as the Gospel was written in Rome, Mark addressed it principally to Roman readers. Hence there are very few Old Testament quotations and allusions; there are also certain Latin words which are to be found in none of the other Gospels, an indication that it was made to appeal to the Roman mind. Mark uses the Roman division of the watches of time, instead of the Jewish division as used, for example, by Matthew. The Gospel for the Roman world would have to present the career of Our Lord as answering the idea of Divine power, work, law, conquest, since the Romans were men of action rather than of thought. Hence Mark presents Christ as the Mighty Worker rather than as the Profound Thinker, the Man Who conquers by doing. His emphasis is on what Our Lord did as the Son of God, rather than on what He said. It was also to be noted that Mark devotes three-eighths of the whole account to the happenings of a single week, wherein Christ met the power of Roman law and the trials and rose triumphantly from the dead. In quick and swift touches, Christ is revealed as the Lord of the world and the Conqueror of the hearts of men, and as establishing an increasing dominion over evil, over nature, and over all powers that oppose Him until at last He rises from the grave.

It is very fitting, therefore, that Mark, who was so much concerned with details in his reporting, should now be buried in one of the most detailed and beautiful churches of Christendom, St. Mark's of Venice.

John. John, the greatest of them all, was by nature much more inclined to take the lead than Peter. There was even a certain intolerance and narrowness in his character. This in part might have been due to the fact that he was better off economically than the other Apostles, inasmuch as his father, Zebedee, a fisherman, had hired servants; socially too, inasmuch as his mother, Salome, was a relative of the Blessed Mother and had enough of the world's goods to minister of her substance to the early church. This impetuosity of John is revealed in his Gospel in almost every single instance in which he is brought to the front, alone or with his brother, James. There is always associated with him some error of perception. John had so much to learn because of exaggeration of tenden-

cies that later on were to make him great. For example, he at
one time was engaged in a dispute with the other Apostles as to
who was the greatest. Our Blessed Lord had to place a child in
the midst of them to teach them the lesson of humility; on
another occasion, jealousy was manifested, as he forbade an
exorcist to cast out devils in the name of Our Lord. Finally,
there was a readiness to violence, as was clear from his attitude
toward a Samaritan village which refused to receive Our Blessed Lord. John asked the Master to rain down fire from
Heaven as Elias did, to wrap the village in flames. It was no
wonder that Our Blessed Lord nicknamed John and his brother
Boanerges, or Sons of Thunder. In this particular instance, the
Son of Thunder wanted a flash of lightning. His conduct was
not evil; it was just inspired by a fiery and zealous nature which
had yet to be tamed.

John learned his lesson when Our Blessed Lord was on His
way to Jerusalem to be crucified. On that occasion, his mother
went to Our Blessed Lord and asked that her two sons, James
and John, should sit at His right and His left when He came
into the Kingdom. Our Blessed Lord asked them if they could
drink the cup of the Passion that He was about to drink. There
was no doubt that John had a loving desire to be near Our
Lord, but his thought was on glory, and not on the Cross. John
was prepared for glory without suffering, in order that he might
have a maximum of grace with a minimum of service. When
Our Blessed Lord told John that the cross of suffering was the
condition of glory, He was not denying John a place in His
Kingdom; He was only showing that the blessing asked for
could not be gained except by a crucifixion.

Up to that moment in the life of John, glory to him was
preferment, a claim, prestige, first place, and ambition. When
Our Lord made him that answer, the mirror in which his own
greatness was reflected was smashed to pieces. The son of
Zebedee died. He exchanged the love of self for love of humanity. He saw clearly that fellowship with the sufferings of Christ
was the condition of sharing in His glory. Here the Saviour set
forth death as the climax of His work, and not teaching; He sets
down the condition in which the fulfillment of John's desire is
possible and then approves that desire.

In the fourteenth year of the reign of Domitian, John was exiled to the Isle of Patmos. As an old man he began to write his Gospel, which was an echo of a harp whose perturbed strings had been smitten by the bloodstained hands of Roman persecutors and then swept by the hand of a mighty inspiration. When it came to his Gospel, he said that his purpose was to declare that Christ is the Son of God, and that, believing, we might have life in His Name. The generation had now lived which had seen God in the flesh. The burning words of the Master had been circulating from home to home and from city to city and from community to community; men were eating the Bread of Life come down from Heaven. St. Paul's Epistles were widely distributed, spreading like a prairie fire from Galilee to Antioch, from Galatia to Ephesus, from Alexandria to Athens and to Rome. The loyal faithful of the Church were already familiar with the synoptic Gospels of Matthew, Mark, and Luke. The catacombs were now being used in the Greco-Roman world, honeycombed "by the faith delivered to the saints."

John addresses his Gospel to all Christian people, reaffirming what was in the other Gospels—that Christ is both true God and true Man, the Word made Flesh, the Eternal in time, Omnipotence in bonds. His Gospel reflects the crisis of his own life, in which he learned the definition of glory. Hence in the first part of the Gospel, John depicts the seven miracles by which Christ presents to the world His glory, which is that of the Son of God; in the last half of the Gospel, John now pictures Our Blessed Lord speaking to His Apostles of that same glory which many men refused to believe, a glory which he identified with his crucifixion. Our Blessed Lord presented the Cross as the very highest moment of His glorification as He is pictured in John as praying, "Father the hour has come, glorify Thy Son."

Out of the lesson which John learned when he asked for earthly glory without the Cross, John now presents the Gospel of the glory which is the Cross as the supreme manifestation of love: "Greater love than this no man hath, that He lay down His life for His friends."

To the credit of John, it must be said that he stood at the foot of the Cross when Our Blessed Lord died. Eight days before he had asked for a place at the right or left side; now he saw those sides occupied by two thieves—and his brother, James, was not there. John could never forget the great lesson that he learned from the Saviour when He spoke of the cup of His Passion. It was, therefore, natural for him to record these words in greater detail than the other Evangelists, for they were related more appropriately to his life. So full was John of this glory which was manifested in the Cross that he ends his Gospel with the words: "There is much else besides that Jesus did; if all of it were put in writing, I do not think the world itself would contain the books which would have to be written."

These are our four writers, and they are available to everyone, free.

† 2 †

Angels

Our modern world does not believe in angels, regarding them as poetical and mythical creatures that tide over the transition from infancy to maturity. The decline of belief in angels does not prove that the world has gotten wiser, but rather that it has become materialistic. The principle reason why angels have lost their following is because angels are created substances of pure intelligence, but devoid of all bodily qualities and characteristics. The modern mind lives in a closed universe in the sense that man is believed to be just an animal devoid of an immortal soul, and with no other purpose in life than to attain security and enjoy pleasure. As the Soviet world is a closed society allowing no influences from the outside world to pass into it except science, which it can turn against the Western world, so the modern minds allow nothing from the spiritual universe to penetrate into its closed circle. Materialism means that people live cramped lives as they live in cramped apartments and crowded highways; materialistic minds breathe in the same air as they breathe out. The result is a suffocation and a stifling of the human spirit.

There are other penalties, too. The first effect of materialism is to be seen in architecture which is devoid of all ornamentation. The building of the United Nations looks like a cracker box with cellophane windows, as do many of the newer types of buildings. When a civilization has faith, matter is used to symbolize the spirit; hence such decorations as gargoyles, phoenixes, wheat, and grapes. When a civilization ceases to believe in the spirit, then there is nothing to represent symbolically, and architecture settles down to the dull, drab line without ornamentation and without reference to another world.

Another effect of materialism is to be seen in the decline of courtesy. There is politeness and decorum and a desire to please others when it is generally recognized that every person bears within himself an image of the Divine. Materialism, denying the supreme worth of the individual, finds him something to be used rather than respected. Recently, on the subway, I got up and gave my seat to a lady who was holding on to a strap. She was rather surprised and said to me, "Why did you do that?" Seeing that she was incapable of understanding a spiritual reason, I said to her, "Madam, I tell you, ever since I was a little boy, I have had an infinite respect for a woman with a strap in her hand."

Though materialism leaves no room for the spiritual and therefore none for angels, it must nevertheless have compensations for its surrender of the infinite. Angels come naturally to a child, because he lives in a dream world and is stardusty from tumbling amidst the spheres. Constantly haunted by the question "Why?" he seeks the infinite and the absolute. When told by his materialistic elders that there is nothing above matter, he must compensate for the loss of the spiritual by fantasies of the imagination such as Space Cadets, Captain Video, Captain Midnight, and Superman. The adult, too, must have his compensations, so he manufactures substitutes such as the "Id" and the inferiority complex, flying saucers, inhabitants of Mars.

The word "angel" is taken from a Greek word, *angelos*, which means messenger. An angel is a creature far below God in dignity and yet far above man, purely spiritual, possessed of an intellect and will, but without a body. When we die, our soul will still be possessed of an intellect and will, but without a body; to that extent it will be like an angel, but the comparison is inexact, inasmuch as our soul always has an aptitude for a body and will recover it in the resurrection; but an angel never had a body, and never will have one as proper to its nature. The Jews believed in angels, considering St. Michael, the Archangel, as the protector of Israel, for so he is revealed in the Old Testament. Moslems believe in angels; Christians believe in angels; and pagans believed in angels. Plutarch, the Greek historian, said, "Alongside of each man there are two angels, one good and one bad." Epictetus said, "God assigns to every man a guardian angel." Seneca and Virgil believed in angels. The oldest representation of an angel is to be found on a slab of limestone about five feet by ten recently found at Ur-Nammu. At the top of the representation is a king in an attitude of prayer, and above him angels are pouring blessings upon his head. This representation dates from the neo-Sumerian period of around two thousand years before Christ. Plato and Aristotle also held that God used angels for the government of the world. The pagan philosophers came to believe in angels because they started with the principle that effects resemble causes; the more perfect the effect, the more it should resemble the cause; therefore there should be spiritual creatures endowed with an intellect and a will, who would be more like God than the stones which merely have existence and plants which merely have life. An angel, having no body, is therefore devoid of parts; hence there is nothing in an angel that can ever come loose. The angel wears a body very much like a waiter wears a dickie. The theme song of an angel is, "I ain't got no body."

An angel may take a body on a special occasion, just as a man may get a new dress suit for a wedding, but the body is taken for our sakes, not for the sake of the angel. When Raphael gave hospitality to Tobias, he said, "I seem indeed to eat and drink with you, but I use an invisible meat and drink which cannot be seen by men." The Archangel Gabriel was not out of breath when he came to Mary in the Annunciation.

There is not room enough in all the world to satisfy the soul of man, but there is room enough in the heart of a man for an angel, for an angel takes no room.

The intelligence of angels. The angelic intelligence is quite different from the human intelligence. The human mind at birth is very much like a blackboard. It is only in the course of time, and thanks to sensible experience, that ideas are written on the human intellect. But the angel does not receive its knowledge from things. Rather, ideas are poured into the angel of God. Man knows from the bottom up; an angel knows from the top down. An angel does not grub in matter, because it has no body. God pours His ideas *intellectually* into angels and *physically* into things. We recover the ideas that God put into things, thanks to our intellect working on sensible experiences. We, therefore, have to unwrap the ideas that God put into things. An angel never has to wait until a package is unwrapped, it already knows what is in things. An angel, therefore, is far more brilliant than man. An angel knows more science than Einstein, more baseball than Leo Durocher, and more jokes than Bob Hope. When an angel has an idea, for example the idea of man, the angel knows every individual man in the world in virtue of that idea. Human beings do not. We just know humanity in general.

There are, however, certain limitations to angelic knowledge. An angel does not know future contingent events, an angel does not know the mysteries of grace, unless God reveals them; and finally an angel does not know the secrets of the heart and the motivations of the will; only God and the psychiatrist know these—or at least some psychiatrists so presume.

The trial of angels. Not all angels are good. The bad angels are those who failed in the trial to which all creation is subjected. Running through the universe is the law that no one shall be crowned unless he has struggled. A man's life on earth is a novitiate, a moment in which he may say "Aye" or "Nay" to this eternal destiny. The angels, too, had to pass a test before they were confirmed in glory. What that test was, we do not know for certain. One of the best guesses is that God revealed to the angels the fact that man would sin through an abuse of his freedom and that God, out of love, would become man in the Person of Christ in order to redeem him. Some of the angels thought that it was unbecoming the dignity of God to descend to lowly human nature; He should have become an angel rather than humiliate Himself to the form and habit of man. Some of the angels affirmed that they would not adore God if He became man. If this be the true test, then they were lost for that sin of rebellion.

Once an angel has made a decision, it can never again change its mind. In this the mind of an angel is very unlike that of a woman. It is said that a woman's mind is cleaner than a man's because she changes it more often. An angel cannot change its mind, because an angel sees the consequences of each and every one of its decisions with the same clarity that we see the principle of contradiction, or the principle that the part can never be greater than the whole. Once we understand the meaning of the word "part" and the meaning of the word "whole," the principle flashes in an irrevocable way that the part is never greater than the whole. An angel sees everything that clearly, and hence its choices cannot be taken back. Man does not see the consequences of his decisions as clearly as an angel does. His choices are confused sometimes through passion and sometimes through ignorance. Hence man can be forgiven seventy times seven, but redemption does not apply to the fallen angels.

Function of guardian angels. Though there are many tasks assigned to the angels, we here limit ourselves to those angels which are called guardian. Among their functions, two may be mentioned:

1. Illumination
2. Protection

Angels can illumine the mind in the way of truth and strengthen the will in the direction of goodness. It is within their power to stimulate our intellect in such a way as to actualize an idea more efficaciously. Though they may inspire the will to goodness, they cannot, however, destroy the human will. That an outside intelligence should affect our own is not surprising. Even in the lower creation, snakes have the power to charm birds although there is no bodily contact; in dreams, images seem to be impressed upon our mind independently of our direction; psychological laboratories are now suggesting such a thing as extrasensory perception, in which there does seem to be the invisible influence of one mind on another, without any exchange of the visible or the audible. A professor illumines the minds of his students, unless he happens to be a poor professor and is merely a textbook wired for sound. How often, too, there is a communication of one person with another person in a room, particularly those who are in love, and no one seems to be conscious of the communication except those two persons. In addition to infusing into our minds good hopes, resolutions, intentions, and aspirations, it may very well be, too, that the function of an angel is also to stir up our souls when we do wrong, causing us anxiety, worry, and distress, so that if we seek not God in the patch of goodness, the angel will worry us until we throw ourselves back again to His embrace.

Every person has a guardian angel, because every person has an immortal destiny and is worth more than the entire universe. In lower nature such as the animal kingdom, it is only the species that are important, for nature seems to be heedless of the number of individuals that perish. But in humanity, it is the person or the individual who has worth; therefore God has provided him with a guardian. To eschew this companionship is to abandon Heaven's help. Man is always better if he lives in companionship with those who have higher ideals; he is always worse when his companionship is with inferiors. He is condemned to the sterility of mediocrity if his association is only with equals. Human nature always does much better when it works under the eye of someone nobler than self. Even the children when they perform a task want to have their mother's eye upon them: "Mama, watch me as I do this." Each human would be nobler in his activity and happier in his heart if, instead of seeking to keep up with the Joneses, he sought to live up the illumination of his own personal angel.

Our Blessed Lord, referring to the guardian angels of children, said, "See to it that you do not treat one of these little ones with contempt; I tell you, they have angels of their own in Heaven, that behold the face of My Heavenly Father continually." Thus the guardian angels of children stand in Heaven with an unclouded vision of the Heavenly Father. Satan, one of the fallen angels, also believes in guardian angels, for in tempting Our Blessed Lord, he said to Him, "If Thou art the Son of God, cast Thyself down to earth; for it is written, He has given charge to His angels concerning Thee, and they will hold Thee up with their hands, lest Thou should chance to trip on a stone."

Those who have raised children are in constant wonder that they ever reach maturity. What is that mysterious power that protects children as they fall out of second- and third-story windows unharmed? When one thinks of the pots and pans that they pull off stoves and of the thousands of falls they have during their infancy and the fires they start, it must be that the Good Lord has given them some very special protection—and this protection we are assured by the Lord Himself is the guardian angel.

Guardian angels should be thought of particularly in relation to aviation. Some people are afraid to fly, which proves they have no trust in the guardian angel, and much less faith in God Himself. The implication in this: "So long as I am here on earth, Oh Lord, You cannot touch me. I am safe; I am the captain and master of my destiny. But once I take a plane and fly, You may be seen lurking behind one of those white clouds, ready to come out, stop the propeller, and send me crashing down to the earth." This is equivalent to calling God a coward, by assuming that He chooses the less safe moments in the air rather than secure moments on earth to summon us to judgment. Naturally, those who believe not in the loving Providence of God never think of His protecting angels who are with us on the land, on the sea, and in the air. Every day we say a prayer to Saint Raphael who is mentioned in the Old Testament as being the traveling companion of Tobias; this prayer is said whether we fly or not, but when we do fly, there is always absolute assurance of protection. Furthermore, if we really love God, we would seek to fly not only to see the more beautiful side of the clouds which the Lord has turned to the heavens, but also in order that in the air we might glorify God as He is glorified on earth.

The reason we do not think of angels is that we do not think of God. If we never think of a boat, or a plane, or a letter of ours going to a tiny little island off the coast of Africa, it is because we never think of that island. If we never think of God, we never think of messengers and their messages coming to us. Just as soon as we cease thinking of ourselves as little tin gods, then we will be more conscious of angels, and invoke their guardianship and their instruction. There may be a public library around the corner from us, but we do not use it, and therefore we are not wise; there may be uranium in the back yard but we do not use a Geiger counter and therefore are not wealthy; there may be a Bible on the shelf but we read it not, and therefore are lacking spiritual inspiration. There are angels near us to guide and protect us, but we do not invoke them. It is not later than we think. It is a bigger world than we think. If we would but stir our soul, we would sprout a wing and discover it to be a wing of an angel of God.

† 3 †

Why Do People Laugh?

There may be the joy of existence among the animals, but the wonderful madness called laughter is found only with man. Nothing in lower creation ever produced anything resembling a laugh. The valleys did not smile and the mountains rock with a laughter. The pony did not titter and the truck horse give a horse laugh; the early hyenas did not grin and the later ones laugh—they only had their mouths open. Crocodiles shed tears—but they do not laugh. One never meets a smile until one comes to man; man "breaks" out into a laugh, for it is a positive break with everything below him in creation; it is a break with the past, it is a break with matter, it is the beginning of the spirit. Man is the only joker in the deck of Nature. Laughter is exclusively human for three reasons, but all are forms of the one basic argument: because he has a soul. In virtue of his spirit, which is different in kind to matter, man

1. Perceives meanings
2. Is capable of introspection, thus seeing not only his own foibles but also those of others
3. Because of the contrast of his body and soul is capable of many incongruities

19

1. *Perception of meanings.* Laughter, from a philosophical point of view, may be explained as the effect of the unexpected juxtaposition of two ideas or the unexpected relationship between two judgments. First, it must be unexpected. That is why we ask before starting a story, "Have you heard this before?" Since an intellectual relationship can be perceived only by man, it follows that man alone can laugh.

Begin with the pun, which has been called the lowest form of humor. Nobody seems to know why it is the lowest form of humor, but the philosophical explanation is that every pun changes the subject with great rapidity. In order to understand a pun, there must be a confrontation of two meanings at one and the same time. One is a common meaning; the other is the remote meaning. One is the real meaning; the other is the departure from that meaning. There is a discovery of resemblance at the same time that there is a difference. Take, for example, the story of a visitor who asked a little girl of six, "What will you do when you get as big as your mother?" "Diet," answered the child. Suppose a dog, a cat, or a canary were in the room at the same time; each would receive exactly the same auditory stimuli, and perhaps better than any human being. Why is it that the canary would not smile, but the visitor perhaps would? It is because the visitor would perceive meaning in the auditory stimuli, that is to say, something more than the mere words. The visitor would see a double meaning in the word big, namely, the "age" meaning, which was the meaning intended, and the "size" meaning, which was the unintended meaning.

But in order to see both meanings at one and the same time, which is the condition of understanding any pun, one must not only be material, but also spiritual. If a box is filled with salt, it cannot be filled with pepper at one and the same time; if the mind is filled only with matter, namely, the auditory sensation of "big," it cannot see the word big in the other sense that produces laughter. The pun, "Many a blonde dyes by her own hand," again involves an unexpected juxtaposition of two words that sound alike but have entirely different meanings. No animal understands meanings or intellectual relationships, therefore no animal laughs.

Perhaps the best answer to be given to those who say that the pun is the lowest form of humor is the classic remark of Oscar Levant: "A pun is the lowest form of humor—when you don't think of it first." It should be remembered, too, that our greatest writer in English was also our greatest punster, namely, Shakespeare. Nor is it to be forgotten that the greatest pun that was ever made was made by the Son of God Himself. He met a man whose name was Simon and He changed his name to Rock, which is the meaning of Peter. When Simon Peter confessed His Divinity, saying, "Thou art Christ, the Son of the living God," Our Blessed Lord answered him, saying, "Thou are the rock, and upon this rock I will build my church and the gates of Hell shall not prevail against it."

2. *Man alone is capable of introspection.* Laughter is also possible because we have a soul which has operations independent of the body. We are able to bend back upon ourselves, look at ourselves as in a mirror, be pleased or angry with ourselves, see ourselves as others see us; nothing material can do that. Because we are spiritual as well as material, we can not only see ourselves as others see us, and therefore perceive our ridiculousness at times, but we are capable of guessing what goes on in the mind of another, thus making room for another kind of laughter. It takes considerable humility, however, to laugh at our own foibles and eccentricities; only the saints ever reach a point where they enjoy having their weaknesses made the subject of laughter. People today generally take themselves too seriously, because they rarely enter into themselves to see the way they are in relation to any other standard than the one of their own making. They judge their todays by yesterdays but not by an eternal standard which begins contrition, humility, and laughter.

Caricature is based on the fact that someone has discovered in us an idiosyncrasy or peculiarity. Let a cartoonist draw a group of twenty persons in a room, concentrating on a humorous aspect of each. It will be found that everyone will think all the caricatures about others are funny, but not the one about himself. Few have the humility of Socrates, who was lampooned in the play *The Clouds* by Aristophanes. Socrates went to the theater and stood up during the entire spectacle, so that everyone could see how true the caricature really was. Mimicry, too, has its foundation in the ability of a human being to introspect both self and another, such as a peculiar way of walking or talking or an affectation.

As the world loses its belief in the spiritual, it also loses an area of humor. The bigger the universe, the deeper the dimension of humor. A decline of a belief in immortality and a future life makes this world much more serious. Certain details of life are subject to satire only in the light of a higher value. The decline of satire both in the theater and in literature is due to a too great immersion in the material. Our Blessed Lord satirized the man who filled his barns because that night his soul was to be required of him. It takes a belief in another world to make this world ridiculous and incongruous. It may very well be that the decline of dialect stories is due to an extreme sensitiveness about nationality. A generation ago, the Irish, the Germans, and the Jews loved to have stories told about them; today, they regard such stories as an insult.

Very few today examine their consciences or practice self-knowledge or do any introspection of the nonpsychoanalytical type. Such egocentrism can never stand off from itself and see itself as it really is. Children are basically egotistic; that is one of the reasons why they hate to be laughed at. Extreme sensitiveness characterizes their every move. The adult who has never grown up to be humble is serious about even his failings. As Swift said, "Satire is a glass wherein beholders generally discover everybody's face but their own." The earth is understood best by looking at the heavens, and the sea is enjoyed best from the shore; so does this life offer light moments when seen *sub specie aeternitatis*.

3. *Incongruity between the higher and the lower values.* The third reason why laughter is possible is because we belong to two worlds; we have a body and a soul; we have our feet on earth, but we dream in the sky. We belong to a world of facts and a world of values; a world of matter and a world of spirit; a world of time and a world of eternity. A purely material world would not be funny, any more than stones are funny. In a world where everything is ridiculous, nothing can be made ridiculous. One cannot unmask a mask. If life is upside down

and there is no telling which is the head and which is the tail, there is no point in pulling the tail. If there is no philosophy of life, no sense of values, no hierarchy of worth, there can be a clash of boredoms, but never humor or comedy. But since we belong to two worlds, it is possible to judge one in the face of the other. Hence, there can be incongruity, contrast, or exaggerated value of the one as against the other, or a diminished value of one in the face of the other. Laughter is often the result of de-gradation or a decline or a falling off of higher values. *It is in the face of a spiritual value that a material value can be ridiculous.* For example, the stink associated with a dead animal is never funny, but if we met a man by the name of Mr. Stinker, it might strike us as very funny. Here a human value of personality is dragged down to the level of the material.

The only thing about which you can make jokes is a serious subject. Funny is the opposite of not funny. The reason there are so many jokes about marriage is because it is a serious subject. Why is it, for example, when we see a tree fall, or a chimney fall, or a plate fall that we do not laugh? Because this is not in relationship to any higher value. Suppose we see a very dignified and cocky man falling on the ice; this is laughable, not just because of the contrast of his assumed dignity and the indignity to which he is now exposed; there is actually a spiritual and moral judgment brought to bear, namely, he ought to fall to humble his pride. Perhaps there is some profound theological relationship to original sin and the Fall of Man in such an event.

Monkeys are funny, not just because they are monkeys, but because, without understanding it, they often give some kind of imitation of man. There is a de-gradation of values in the antics of monkey. Parrots, in like manner, are capable of giving amusement because they say words which have meaning and yet they do not understand the meaning. A dog who belongs to a friend of mine was one day stopped by a drunk in the street. Because the drunk was reeling, the dog had a sense that the actions were rather abnormal for a human being; so the dog turned his head and looked up—half backing away from inebriate. The alcoholic, justifying himself, said, "It's alright, buddy, I know I am drunk." Sheer imitation without establishing a contrast through exaggeration or debasement would not be funny. Nobody laughs at a man on the street with his hat cocked on the side of his head, but everyone would laugh at a bishop in church whose miter was crooked. Here there is a too rapid descent of the spiritual into the material and the incongruity would produce laughter. Dogs walking up and down the street never creat laughter, but let a dog walk down the aisle of a church, and everyone thinks it is funny. There is nothing funny about seeing a man running at a track meet, but there is something funny about seeing a man run after a silk hat. There is nothing amusing about trying to see a man get fish out of a pond, but there can be something amusing and laughable about seeing a man trying to get a piece of cork out of a glass—maybe because this is a de-gradation of his vocation to be a fisher of men. There is nothing very funny about taking a drowning boy out of the water, but a man trying to get a drawer that is stuck out of bureau or desk can sometimes be rather laughable to those who are watching, particularly if it be an atheist; he who does not believe in God now makes an affirmation of a belief in God, the existence of hell, and Divine judgments. Jokes about clergymen are numerous because they are supposed to be dignified and scholarly. As Chesterton says, "Bishops' garters are very funny, but some are making fun of the garters while forgetting the Bishops."

The mother-in-law also admits of this conflict of a world of facts and values. People thought it amusing that Samuel Butler once said of a certain woman that she should never have been a mother, but she would have made a great mother-in-law. However, it should be remarked in defense of all mothers-in-law that St. Peter remained the truest friend of Our Blessed Lord, despite the fact that Our Lord cured his mother-in-law. Why is it that Communism can never make any jokes about itself? Because it denies a higher set of values, namely, the spirit by which the material might be judged. Materialism is a very serious business; it is possible for us in democracies to laugh at Communism, simply because we have other values than the material and the economic.

Laughter, it has been said, involves a contrast between a world of fact and a world of value. But if the incongruity or contrast or degeneration of values is carried beyond a certain point, there is no laughter, but rather villainy and cruelty. Hence Aristotle says, in his *Poetics,* that laughter should never give pain to others. Teasing which at first produces laughter can, if carried too far, evoke a sympathy for the one who is being ridiculed. Where there is a complete destruction of values, there can even be tears. The defects of others never constitute a subject of humor because they are not responsible for their decline from the norm. To laugh, for example, at a cripple is just the same as beating him with his own crutches. A person who pretends to be sick is funny, but a truly sick person, regardless of his actions, is never an occasion for fun, because there is a danger of the great value of human life being destroyed.

Man laughs because he has a soul or a spirit. Hence, the more spiritual a person is, the more enjoyment there is in life. In this sense, humor is closely related to faith; it bids us not take anything too seriously. There is an anticipation of heaven in pure fun, because in heaven, we will have attained our purpose and thus can enjoy a kind of purposeless living, like a man who has worked hard to build a house, and now no longer wants to build another, but just to live in it: "In My Father's house, there are many mansions." Sheer nonsense, such as "What did moths eat before Adam and Eve wore clothes?" has no purpose except pure enjoyment. It is therefore like the fugues of Bach, which, it seems, could go on forever, or the purposeless joy of looking at the formation of clouds in the skies; or the purposeless play of children, such as throwing stones in a pond. It is like contemplation, which the greatest philosopher who ever lived compared to play, because it gave pleasure, and because it had no other purpose than itself. The joy of children's play is the key to eternal laughter; that is why Our Lord said that we could not enter heaven unless we became like little children.

"Look for me in the nurseries of heaven."

† 4 †

Life of Karl Marx

Our Blessed Lord said, "Out of the abundance of the heart the mouth speaketh." What is important is not always *what* a man says, but *why* he says it. A man speaks according to his spiritual condition. The heart is to be found in the deliverances of the tongue and the pen. If a man does not live according to Truth, he will adjust an idea to the way he lives; thus a philosophy of life is born from his behavior. This is particularly true in the case of Karl Marx, the founder of Communism.

Karl Marx, the so-called "defender of the proletariat," or the worker, was not of proletariat origin. Though he is pictured by his followers as a defender of social justice, he did not come to that position because he was distressed at seeing the poverty of others, or because he himself was in poverty, or because he was shocked at economic injustice. His economic theory of Communism came relatively late in his life. Much of the philosophy that he developed is to be found in his heart and in his behavior for the first few decades of his life.

Karl Marx was born in Trier, Germany, May 5, 1818. His father, Heinrich Marx, and his wife, Henrietta, were members of the respectable Jewish middle class in the Rhineland. The father, a distinguished lawyer, came from a family of rabbis who had been supplying the synagogues of the city for 150 years. One of his ancestors, Josef Ben Cohen, was Rabbi of Cracow in the sixteenth century. At the University of Padua hung a portrait of another ancestor, a rabbi who was one of the most illustrious minds of his time. The mother of Marx, Henrietta Pressburger, also descended from a long line of Jewish rabbis.

Heinrich Marx was baptized in the autumn of 1816 and changed his name to Herschel. In August, 1824, Herschel Marx appeared in a Christian church surrounded by seven children, all of whom were baptized. The reason for the baptism of his children was not because of any persecution, because the emancipation of the Edict of 1812 gave the Prussian Jews their full civil liberty; nor was it because Marx himself was convinced of Christianity, for he rather adhered to the *Aufklarung,* rationalistic, and free-thought philosophy of Europe because of the affection that he had for Frederick the Great. The real reason was that Herschel Marx was a Prussian at heart, an attachment which had to be concealed, because after the French Revolution the city of Trier lost its prestige as a capital and became a part first of the French Republic and later on of the Empire. The Empire collapsed at Waterloo with the defeat of Napoleon. After the Congress of Vienna, the city was returned again to Prussia. Prussian soldiers now began to walk the streets, while the arms of the Hohenzollern king appeared on the public buildings. Immediately after the return of Trier to the Prussians, Marx wanted above all things else to declare his affiliation to Prussia; the best way to do it was to join the Evangelical Established Church of the Kingdom of Prussia. That was why he was baptized in 1816 and why his children later on were baptized in the year 1824. The mother of Karl Marx was baptized some time later.

Baptism does something to a human being, something akin to changing a crystal into a living cell. It does actually make a creature into a child of God. Born of parents, we are like our parents; born of God in Baptism, we participate in the Divine Nature. This new life of grace in the soul in many people may lie dormant, just as God may give a talent for music though one may never exercise that talent. If, however, the human will turns against the gift, then something happens in the soul. If the stomach cannot assimilate the food which is put into it and which was meant to nourish it, the stomach may turn against the food, revolt against it, and the food itself may cause its own disorders. In the soul, however, there can be no such thing as spiritual indigestion unless it is willed deliberately. When the will turns against the gift of God, then grace in the soul becomes something like ground glass in the stomach. As a lover may hate the gift of the beloved whom he has spurned, so, too, the soul can revolt and turn against God and become worse on account of the gift. *Corruptio optimi pessima,* "The corruption of the best is the worst."

Karl Marx saw his family making a plaything of religion and turn from Judaism to Christianity, not because of religious conviction, but because of political preferment. As Judaism was never practiced before, so Christianity would not be practiced now. Karl Marx grew up *déraciné,* uprooted, without ties to race, country, Israel, or Christianity but hating all four. Is it any wonder that such a man should later on call religion the "opium of the people" since in his own life and his family, religion was used as a dope to put to sleep, not only Israel, but Christ?

The tension that was already in the soul of young Marx manifests itself in egotism, which, the father told him in one of his letters, "is your ruling passion." On another occasion, his father told him that he hoped that no "demonic spirit" would win him away from what is pure and human. What was basic in the life of Marx was his hatred of religion. After studying for a while in the University of Bonn, well supplied with money, he goes to Berlin, where he decides to become a poet as he fills four notebooks full of poems, the first one of which is called "The Book of Love, I," Then "The Book of Love, II." His father, concerned about the money he was giving to Karl, asked him to turn to something more practical. Three years after his father's death, he still remained in Berlin, being supported by the small capital which was left to his mother. During these three years he spent most of his time with some intellectual Bohemians who united together to form what was known as the Professors Club. The aim of the club was the furthering of atheism. Discussed at this club were such subjects as the *Life of Jesus* by David Friedrich Strauss, which attempted to empty the Gospels of their historical value; the members, too, liked the dialectics of Hegel, which seemed to satisfy the tension that already existed in the soul of Marx. Hegel held that thought is based upon contradiction; first the affirmation of an idea, second the negation of an idea, and third the synthesis resulting from the conflict of the first two. Though there was little of the idea of God in Hegel, Marx and the other members of the club felt that there was too much of God; Marx one day startled the whole group by affirming that Hegel was an atheist.

Another member of the club, who had received his doctorate, asked Marx "to pass a stupid examination" in order to receive his doctor's degree. Marx wrote on dialectics, his thesis being a comparison of the system of Democritus and Epicurus. It was written in a style which already reflected the tension in his soul, the second sentence contradicting the first, and the third sentence uniting the first two in some kind of presumed higher thought. The thesis ended with the words "I hate all the gods." Marx sent his thesis to the University of Jena and received a kind of mail-order Ph.D. degree after taking the examination by correspondence.

Marx now decided with a friend of his named Bruno Bauer to found a magazine entitled *Archives of Atheism*. Bauer's plan was as follows: he would become a professor of theology at the University of Bonn, where he would teach atheism instead of theology. Marx, later on, was to follow him. The theological faculty at Bonn discovered the Fifth Column activity of Bauer and refused to accept him. Marx, therefore, was unable to worm his way into the theological faculty. He blamed his failure upon a conspiracy of hidden sinister forces, and his hatred of religion became intensified.

Another interest of the Professors Club was the appearance of the work of Ludwig Feuerbach, who attacked Christianity on the basis of materialism. The thesis of Feuerbach was that man created gods by projecting the idea of infinity, which was man's rightful attribute, to an imaginary deity. It is not going to be a long step for anyone now to argue that one can project a social idea or economic theory into history. This is precisely what Marx did. Uniting the dialectics of Hegel to the materialism of Feuerbach, he projected into history his dialectical materialism, pretending it to be the law of nature, the law of history, and the law of social order.

Marx decided to "bring atheism to the people." To this end, he briefly became editor of the *Rhenish Gazette*. At this time he had no interest in economics and was certainly far from Communism. One of the Paris newspapers ridiculed some articles of his and his associates, saying that they who were the offspring of wealthy families were wasting their time with Communist snobbery at the expense of their fathers' bank accounts. Marx answered and said he "could not even grant any theoretical value to Communism, much less desire its practical realization, or even consider it possible."

Marx was not first a Communist and then an atheist; he was first an atheist, then a Communist. Communism was merely the political expression of his atheism. As he hated God, so would he hate those who would own property. As he put it: What atheism is to thought, that Communism is to social action. The intrinsic relationship he explained as follows: "Communism begins where atheism begins." When a man is spiritually uprooted through atheism, he is prepared to become economically uprooted by the destruction of private property. Communism was not born out of thinking; it was born out of hatred: a hatred for what a man *is,* namely, a creature of God, a hatred of what a man *has,* namely, property, the economic guarantee of liberty. Funnel both of these hatreds into a social theory, and you have the philosophy of Communism.

Marx's theory of value. When Karl Marx came to England to live after having married Jenny von Westphalen, he developed what was known as the labor theory of value, which became the bedrock of Communist economics. In ordinary speech, the word *value* is applied to those things which satisfy our needs, such as chalk, blackboards, bread, kneeling benches, and cheese. The value of things is determined by many factors, for example, scarcity, usefulness, subjective association such as the gift from a friend, symbolic value, etc.; Marx set aside all these and other considerations and took the too simple view that the value of anything depends upon the labor time embodied in it. *Labor* is the sole source of *value*.

This is not true; pearls are not valuable because men dive for them; men dive for pearls because pearls are valuable. If labor is the unique source of value, it follows that the capitalist who provided the raw material, the factory, the methods of production, and even the ideas for transforming the raw material is really "exploiting" labor. From this it follows that capital must be done away with and all property put into the hands of the State, which will be under the dictatorship of the proletariat.

Marx's life began with an inconsistency, and now we see it reappearing again. He who developed the labor theory of value, never labored; he who glorified work as the source of value, never worked. What is the peculiar psychological perversity in a man which makes him espouse the opposite of the way he lives? Maybe Marx did it to justify his conscience for not working. At the Universities of Bonn and Berlin he was supported by his father, rather lavishly. At the age of twenty-four, his mother insisted that he go to work to support himself; his sister Sophie told him that he was a parasite on the family, as they sacrificed to give him everything, while they had little.

When he went to London, outside of earning a few dollars over a brief space of time as a correspondent for the *New York Tribune,* he was supported most of his life by his friend Friedrich Engels, the son of a wealthy manufacturer of Manchester. His wife begged him to work as silverware and clothing were pawned, but he went off to the British Museum to write a work on the labor theory of value which later on appeared under the title of *Das Kapital.* His wife was so disgusted with him that she once said, "Karl, if you had only spent more time making capital instead of writing about it, we would have been better off." He received an advance of $300 for his work on *Das Kapital,* but he was writing it from 1844 to 1867. It was the first money he had earned since his correspondence job with the newspaper. The sales of his book were only two hundred copies in one year; this he blamed on "mealy-mouthed babblers of vulgar economy." Engels sent him as much as $1,825 a year, which was considerable in 1850. Marx received an inheritance of $650 from his wife's mother and on another occasion received $800 from an uncle, but the money disappeared, and his wife knew not where.

Rather than work, he made his first visit to his mother after not having seen her in twenty years, and the sole purpose of the visit was to get money. He wrote back to his wife, "She does not want to hear a word about money but she destroyed the I.O.U's that I made out to her; that is the only pleasant result of the two days I spent with her." Returning to London, he said that the old lady could not give him much money.

Marx then hired a lawyer in order to get from his mother a share of the money he would receive when she died. He actually received about six thousand in gold and francs. In 1862, he went to Holland to get more money from his uncle, who told him to get a job, but Marx still refused to work.

All the time that Engels was supporting him, Engels was living with a common-law wife whose name was Mary Burns. In January, 1863, Mary suddenly died of a heart attack. Engels wrote to announce the tragic news to Marx, and Marx answered, "The devil knows there is nothing now but ill luck where we are; I simply don't know any more where to turn. My attempts to rake up money in France and Germany have failed, besides the children have no shoes or clothing to go out in." He then asked Engels for more money.

Engels received the letter before Mary was in her grave; he answered Marx, saying, "All my friends, including bourgeois acquaintances, have shown me on this occasion, which was bound to touch me very closely, more friendship and sympathy then I could expect. You found the moment well chosen to advertise the superiority of your cold philosophy; so be it." But Engels still continued to support Marx.

Toward the end of his life there came to London a young man by the name of Le Moussu who commanded the firing squad which shot the Archbishop of Paris in the uprising of the Commune. He invented a copying machine and went into partnership with another man in the hopes of giving an English translation of *Das Kapital* to exploit his patent. When the partner of Le Moussu died, Marx, who insisted all during his life that the only value a thing had was the labor involved, now decided to become a capitalist. He went into the printing business, stole the patent of Le Moussu, and took over the firm as head capitalist. Le Moussu refused; the case was brought to court. Marx refused to swear on the Bible; he said he would touch it as Mephistopheles might touch it. Marx lost the case. Marx lived to see two of his daughters commit suicide and then in 1883 he was laid in unconsecrated ground in Highgate Cemetery, London.

This is the biography of the founder of Communism, but it is also the biography of Communists. As the Christian exemplifies Christ, so Communism leaves its Marx on every follower. Communists are not born of a love of a social justice. Scrutinize their hearts and it will be discovered that their Communism is born, sometimes of an uneasy conscience, which is the result of bad behavior, which evil conscience is requited for the moment by a hatred of God and religion; other times, it is inspired by a hidden avarice or greed. In some of the rich, this manifests itself by the espousal of Communism to "justify" ill-gotten goods or else to salvage possessions when the Revolution comes; in the poor who, like Marx, dislike work, it reveals itself in a lust for the possessions of others through a revolution which transfers booty and lust from another's pocket into their own. No more miserable, unhappy, distraught, and disturbed people exist in the world than Communists. Did they but know it, their unhappiness is due to the Finger of God stirring their souls, making them restless.

Communists! I know your philosophy better than most of you—I have read all of Marx, Lenin, and Stalin and your Party reports! I have brought peace and happiness to many of your members and Party leaders by encouraging a response to the Finger of God. You have the fire of zeal but not the Truth; we of the Western world have the light of Truth but not the fire of zeal. Bring your flames to our light, and we will bring our light to your flames, and we can enthrone "peace," which is the tranquillity of order.

† 5 †

The Atomic Bomb

History of atoms. About 400 B.C. a Greek philosopher, Democritus, asked himself the question, "Could one take a piece of matter, e.g., a stone, and cut it into smaller and smaller pieces until one reached a point where it could not be cut any more?" His answer was in the affirmative. Since the Greek prefix for "not" is *a-* and the Greek work for "to cut" is *temmein,* the Greeks called the uncuttable, or indivisible, piece of matter an "atom."

From that time on until the present century, atoms were supposed to be indestructible homogeneous little pellets or billiard balls with the same consistency throughout, like jelly; they were the permanent bricks out of which the universe was made. The entire universe was thought to be composed of these small invisible and indivisible particles. When new things were formed, atoms were said to come together like the flock of birds at feeding time; when things disintegrated, atoms fell apart like the birds dispersing.

Science today has found out that the atom is not just a solid piece of matter; rather, it is mostly space in which there is electricity or light. Matter is light. There are two kinds of light

34

in the world: one is bottled light; the other is un-bottled light. Bottled light is matter, such as hinges, doors, and sealing wax. Unbottled light is illumination, such as we find in a candle or a bulb. The whole universe is light, either potential or actual. That is why Sir James Jeans in his work. *The Universe Around Us,* said that the most scientific and accurate description that has ever been given of creation is that found in Genesis: God said, "Let there be light, and light was made."

The inside of an atom is made up of positive and negative charges of electricity: for example, in a hydrogen atom there is one positive charge, the proton, in the center, or what is called the nucleus, and one negative charge, the electron, in the outer shell. The atom is very much like the solar system. In the solar system, the sun is the center, and around about the sun revolve the planets: Mercury, Venus, the Earth, Mars, Jupiter, Saturn, Uranus, and Neptune. The atom is a minature solar system inasmuch as it has a nucleus, which corresponds to the central sun, and electrons, which correspond to the revolving planets.

It must, however, be pointed out that the atom is not exactly like the solar system; there are several differences.

In the solar system, the planetary bodies are held together by gravitation; the atoms are held together by an electrical field. Since an electrical field is much stronger than a gravitational field, it follows that in the world of atoms we shall meet energies that will surpass those in the solar system millions of times. A second difference is that in the solar system the sun is larger than any of the planets. The nucleus of the atom, however, differs little in size from its "planets." The "planets," or electrons, of an atom travel much more quickly than the solar planets. An electron could cross the United States, in a straight line, in less than ten seconds.

Size of an atom. The diameter of a nucleus is one-millionth of a millionth of an inch. If each person on earth were as tiny as an atom, we could all fit into a space smaller than a point of a pin. A spoonful of coffee contains about 50,000,000,000,000,000,000 atoms. No one has ever seen an atom, and probably no one ever will. We know the atom only through its effects; we know God also through creation, its order and its laws.

We said the atom was a kind of miniature solar system. The sun releases energy or light to the earth, it does this by splitting its atoms, though the process is slower in the sun than in a bomb. The sun loses about 240 million tons every minute to service our earth, but this need not frighten us, for the sun still has over 30 billion years yet to go.

Some of the energy that is in the atom could be released, provided we could produce enough heat. In order to light a cigarette, we need a match; and to light an atomic bomb we also need a match. To drive two hydrogen atoms together requires an enormous amount of energy or heat—the estimate is between 20 million to 100 million degrees centigrade.

The lighting of the atom can be done in two ways, just as gasoline can be ignited in two ways. One way is to put a match to the gasoline tank; then we have an explosion. The other way is to vaporize the gasoline through a carburetor, igniting a controlled part of it with a spark from a magneto; the explosive energy of gasoline is thus utilized for peaceful purposes.

The atom can be lighted so as to create an explosion; then we have the atomic or hydrogen bomb. But the lighting can also be controlled; this is done by a nuclear reactor which controls the chain reaction, so that what takes place in a millionth of a second in a bomb now will take place in a longer period. A nuclear reactor corresponds to the carburetor in an automobile. Thanks to nuclear reactions, we now have a submarine and a city in the United States lighted by controlled atomic energy.

How much energy is released by either the fission or the fusion of an atom. Matter and energy were formerly considered to be two totally different things. Now we know that matter is "condensed" energy and energy is matter "exploded" into motion or radiation.

We have many formulas for translating one thing into another; for example, when we go to France we translate dollars into francs. We weigh on a European scale, and we translate a kilogram into 2.2 pounds and an inch into 2.5 centimeters. Einstein has given the formula for translating energy into mass and mass into energy. The formula is

$$E = MC^2$$

E stands for energy, which is measured in terms of ergs. An erg is the equivalent of the amount of energy required to wink. *M* is mass in terms of grams. There are about 45 grams in a pound. *C* means *celeritas,* the Latin for speed. *C* here stands for the velocity of light in centimeters per second, which in round numbers is about 30 billion centimeters a second.

The amount of energy, therefore, that we get out of anything is mass in grams multiplied by the speed of light squared. Now the speed of light squared is 9 followed by twenty zeros. In the fission of a uranium nucleus, one-tenth of 1 percent is converted into energy. The entire mass is never converted into energy. Translating this into simple language, suppose we had a piece of matter the size of a shotgun pellet. Our problem is how much energy could be released. The answer is energy enough to equal the output of all the power stations of the world in one single day. Conversely, if we took the electrical output of all power stations of the world and turned it back into matter, we would discover that it would be about the size of a piece of buckshot. Another way of understanding this would be to take a parking ticket which is put on your automobile by a policeman. How much energy in terms of ergs could you get out of that parking ticket if you could release it by fission or fusion? It would probably be enough to run all the automobiles of the world for several days. The atomic bomb which was dropped on Hiroshima was equivalent to 20,000 tons of TNT. The newer bombs which combine fission and fusion of uranium 238 have an explosive force that is equal to 10 million to 20 million tons of TNT. The Hiroshima bomb killed between 70,000 and 90,000 people and injured about 100,000.

There are many effects which follow the explosion of an atomic bomb, such as fire, heat, nuclear radiation, and radioactivity, which in turn can affect the earth, water, and air. For the first time in history there is a possibility of man using an instrument from which there is no escape. The hydrogen bomb can also increase its deadly effects through "rigging." If a hydrogen bomb is encased in steel, it will do far less damage than if it were encased in cobalt. Cobalt becomes quickly radioactive, and each element made radioactive becomes radioactive in its turn. In order to understand the effect of radioactivity, it may be recalled that radium is used in treating cancer cells, but it could also kill, if not properly administered, healthy cells and even a patient. One bomb encased in cobalt could release into the atmosphere the equivalent of nearly 5 million pounds of radium, which could destroy all life within thousands of miles. The new H bomb nonrigged could destroy everything within an area of 300 square miles, and as an incinerator it could burn everything within 1,200 square miles. When one realizes that 27 per cent of the population of the United States is in forty cities, it can be readily understood how 50 million Americans could be incinerated in a few minutes in atomic warfare.

Atomic scientists have also warned of the effect of radioactivity on the begetting of human life. A Nobel prize winner, Hermann J. Muller, said, "Atomic Warfare may cause as much genetic damage spread over future generations as the direct harm done to the generation exposed." Another geneticist, Alfred H. Sturtevant, says, "The last H Bomb test alone probably will produce more than seventy human mutations which are likely to produce large numbers of defective individuals in the future." Radiation destroys chromosomes and even changes the chemical structure of the genes, which mutations can show up for generations.

Before the hydrogen bomb was ever exploded, Einstein said, "The hydrogen bomb appears on the public horizon as an attainable goal . . . if successful, radioactive poisoning of the atmosphere and hence annihilation of all life on earth has been brought within the range of technical possibilities." Pius XII, in 1943, two years before the atomc bomb was exploded on Hiroshima, warned that a catastrophe of the entire planet would follow upon the explosion of atomic bombs. The second warning came in 1954, when he said that it was possible to exterminate all animal and vegetable and human life over vast areas of the earth. Sir Robert Robertson, president of the British Association for the Advancement of Science, warns that the bigger explosions of hydrogen bombs may set off a thermonuclear reaction on land and on the ocean so as even to destroy the earth. In 1949, Einstein was asked what would be the effect of the Atomic Age. He said, "Come back in twenty years." That would be in 1969.

Go back to 1869, when there was a dinner conversation in Paris, recorded in the *Journal* of the Goncourt brothers. Pierre Berthelot, the famous French scientist who was at the dinner, explained that science had just begun to lisp the alphabet of destruction. He predicted that, in one hundred years, "man would know of what the atom was constituted and would be able at will to moderate, extinguish, and light up the sun as if it were a gas lamp." The Goncourt brothers raised no objection but stated, "We have a feeling that when this time comes to science, God with his white beard will come down to earth, swinging a bunch of keys and will say to humanity the way they say at five o'clock: 'Closing time, gentlemen,' and then we will have to start over again." And 1969 is twenty years after Einstein said, "Come back in twenty years."

In 1953, Churchill said, "When the advance of destructive weapons enables everyone to kill everybody else, no one will want to kill anyone at all." In March, 1945, Leo Szilard sent a memorandum to President Roosevelt in which he discussed the possibility of persuading the Russians to accept some kind of atomic control. He felt the best way to do this was to explode a very powerful atomic bomb. "As to our chances of persuading the Russians to accept mutual control, much may depend on the proper timing of our approach to Russia; it would appear that such an approach would have to be made *immediately after we demonstrated the potency of atomic bombs.*" The argument of Szilard that we should immediately explode an atomic bomb and then induce Russia to talk peace is not very sound, for several reasons:

It ignores history. Every time a new weapon of war has come into being, there have been those who said it would outlaw war. This happened when dynamite was discovered, when the Maxim gun was invented, when dreadnoughts were launched, at the close of World War I, after the use of poison gas. The argument was that violence is a mutual deterrent; hence in America we labored under the illusion that World War I was the "war to end all wars." Man always lives under the false notion that there can be some other basis for peace than the moral and spiritual basis.

A second fallacy in the argument is the belief that the demonstration of physical power will beget moral opinion. It is true that, if the two belligerents in the quarrel are fixed in power and size, the demonstration in power in the one will certainly develop a fear of that power in the other. If a giant drives his bare first through a barn door to prove his might, a midget will be convinced that he should never attack the giant. But nations are not like giants and midgets. Giants and midgets cannot change their stature; but a midget nation as regards an atomic pile can become a giant. Furthermore, the presently weaker nation through the demonstration of power may be impelled to work more ardently until it can overcome the giant. The show of force did not prevent the Russians from taking China or Northern Korea or Northern Vietnam. Will the show of force prevent them from taking the world?

The morality of atomic bombs. Is it permitted to use atomic bombs in war? This is a question that has not boldly been faced, but it must be; and its solution is to be found in the application of moral and spiritual principles.

War may be either aggressive or defensive.

Should the atomic bomb be used in an aggressive war? No! Wars previously were limited geographically and in their objective. Today, an aggressive war would not be just a war against a nation, but a world war or total war. To start such a war, which would endanger all humanity, cannot be justified; much less can atomic bombs be justified in such a war.

May an atomic bomb be used in a *defensive* warfare? The answer is in the affirmative, but only provided three conditions are fulfilled:

1. When there has been a very grave injustice inflicted on a nation.

2. When it is the sole and unique means of legitimate defense.

3. When its effects can be controlled or limited to military objectives. If it is used for the extermination of whole populations, then its use becomes immoral and is to be condemned. In this case, the bomb would not be a defense, but the annihilation of human life. No more violence may ever be used than that which is necessary to vindicate a right. It is not permitted to

shoot a man who owes a dime. The incineration of millions of noncombatants and the endangering of life on earth is the use of a violence far in excess of the defense that any political right demands. *The good to be won must always outweigh the evil which it may occasion.* Cutting off a head will cure a headache, but the remedy is too evil in comparison with the good. No one, just to vindicate the right of free speech, may shout "Fire" in a theater, which may cause a riot in which hundreds are killed.

In the light of the above, it may be concluded that the atomic bomb may not be used even in defensive warfare, because the conditions for its legitimate use cannot be fulfilled. One night the lieutenants of Alexander the Great came to him and told him that the Persian Army was asleep. "Attack now and you will win." Alexander answered, "It is not fair to fight at night." It is night—all over the world. It is not fair to use atomic bombs "at night."

† 6 †

How We Are Torn

Compulsion I

"I am a compulsive drinker." "She is a compulsive eater."
"I don't know what made me do it; I just heard a voice."
These are the excuses one hears daily, implying that the will is
no longer free, but as if under the direction of another.

Is there such a thing as compulsion? Definitely. How does it
come about? Generally through three stages: consent, act and
habit. Every person has buried in his subconsciousness certain
powers, capacities or impulses given for his perfection. One
refers to our body, the other to our mind, and the last to things
outside the body and mind. The first is sex or the creative
impulse; the other is a desire for power, e.g., through a search
for truth or the pursuit of a talent or the right use of power. But
outside of the body and the mind there are things. The person
is finally driven to possess property. Just as the will is free
because a man can call his soul his own, so property is external
and an economic guarantee of human freedom.

Each of these impulses is capable of being perverted. Fire on
the hearth is good, but fire in the clothes closet is not. The sex
instinct can be distorted into license and perversion. In that

case, the other person is really not loved, but is used. One drinks the water; one forgets the glass. Hidden in our nature is a lot of flammable material which is not ignited except by some suggestion from without, with the consent of the will. External influences only tempt; they do not compel. There is no inseparable connection between the two. When Joseph was tempted by Potiphar's wife he said, "How can I do this great wickedness and sin against God?"

The mind's desire for knowledge and truth can be perverted by each person saying to himself, "There will be no measure of truth or knowledge outside of me. Whatever I decide to be true is true. I make the truth. I make the law. I am my own creator. I am my own savior." The drive for the possession of things can be turned into avarice, greed, selfishness and the refusal to help the poor.

When does the good impulse become tempted? It becomes tempted generally by a solicitation from without. For example, the sex impulse might be perverted by a picture, a book, a person. There is no perversion at this particular point; there is only a *suggestion*. This is what is called temptation to do something immoral. No temptation to do evil is wrong in itself; it is only the *consent* which is wrong.

It has been said that it is wrong to repress our impulses. No! Repression is not always wrong. As a matter of fact, every expression of something good, e.g., to give food to a hungry person, is a repression of selfishness.

When an outside evil pleasure is presented, our nature exaggerates the proportions of everything, it shows the pleasure or the profit through a magnifying glass, multiplied by desire and expectation. One can imagine a mountain of gold, but one can never see a mountain of gold. What the imagination does is to present things to the mind not *as they are,* but as the mind would *have them to be.* Notice that all love songs are songs of expectation. Nothing cheats a man as much as expectation, which promises high but performs nothing.

The desire to pervert our good impulses means that the subjective and the objective meet; that which before was only within the heart now begins to feel the touch and the allure of something outside. As Shakespeare said:

How oft the sight of means to do ill deeds
Make deeds ill done!

After the consent of the will to do what is wrong, comes the deed. As the boy grows into a man, so the will grows into the act. Once the wrong act is done, there follows the uneasiness and remorse which is actually God calling the soul back to itself. The act repeated many times turns into habits. They are like tiny strands of silk, any one of which can be readily broken, but when woven day after day, they become a great chain which no giant can break. Habits tend to create or strengthen an attitude and disposition. They become so very natural that we are hardly conscious of them, whether good or bad. All the good things lie downstream, and all we have to do is just float like a log. When finally the habit creates a rut in our brain so that we automatically respond to any temptation, we have what is called "compulsion."

Compulsion II

It has been stated that flammable material exists on the inside of every human being. For example, the righteous use of sex could be perverted into grossness; a desire for perfection could turn one into a tyrant; and the desire for property as the extension of oneself, into a miser. The stages by which one advances into compulsion are: first, the consent of the will to any temptation; next the act which is the result of the temptation; and, finally, the habit itself. It takes many acts to make a habit, as it takes many strands of flax to make a rope.

Habits are good as well as bad. How weary our brain would be if we had to relearn playing the piano each time we sat down to it, or if we had to go through the laborious process of learning to write when we composed a letter. In the case of evil habits, such as alcoholism, the energy which once went into the will to prevent an excess now goes into the habit itself to enforce it. Conscience, which at first registered a protest against an evil action such as hurting a neighbor, becomes dulled from abuse. It is very much like the spring on a screen door during the summertime; it loses its resiliency and ability to close to keep out flies. Good acts make virtue easier, and evil acts make vice eaiser. The hedge broken down is easier to get through. The drops of water flowing through a dike can eventually end in a flood.

How habits eventually lead to compulsion may be illustrated by the parable of the trees of the forest who had a solemn parliament in which they decided to enact some laws against the wrongs which the ax had done them. They finally agreed that no tree would lend wood as a handle for an ax under the pain of being outlawed by the other trees. The ax without a handle traveled up and down the forest and begged for wood from cedar, ash, oak and elm, but no one would lend him a chip. At last he went to the briars near the trunks of the trees and said to the trees that these shrubs were sucking away the chemicals of the soil, and were also obscuring the glory of the fair trees. The trees agreed to give him a handle to cut down the shrubs, but when the ax got the handle, he cut the trees down also.

When a strong man has a palace that is well defended, he can keep his goods in peace. But when one stronger than he attacks the palace, then he loses his goods and also his liberty. In like manner, there eventually comes to some habitual practice of vice what is known as compulsion. Within the course of one evening, two young mothers in an Eastern city were assaulted by a man who broke down the front door, saying, "I am a compulsive sex maniac." There are five million alcoholics in the United States, most of whom would say, "I can't help it, I am a compulsive drinker. The sight of alcohol triggers me, and I have no power to resist."

It is at this point that psychiatrists and social workers and others say with some degree of justice that such people are sick. Indeed they are sick, but they are not sick in the same way as a person with cancer who never willed that the cancer virus should enter his body or that it should be multiplied within his body as a kind of a habit. But all who suffer from a so-called compulsion have entered into this state as a result of successive re-acts, until a point was reached where, as a great Russian writer has said, "unlimited freedom leads to unlimited tyranny."

What must be stressed is that no human will is ever completely ruined by a force on the outside. It can, like a muscle, be cut successively by a knife until the limb drops helpless. What is strange about the compulsion is that although the pleasure attached to the indulgence lessens with each successive indulgence, the power of compulsion increases. The energy that once went into the enjoyment now goes into forging new links in a chain which can be broken only with the greatest difficulty.

Compulsion III

We have explained how successive acts can become habits, and how evil habits can eventually create compulsions in which one justifies himself, saying, "I cannot help it; I am a compulsive drinker," or "I am a compulsive sex maniac," or "I am a compulsive kleptomaniac." What emotions and feelings are associated with those under compulsion? First, almost all generally excuse themselves of any guilt. The blame is outside of them, not inside. This has been the story of human nature from the beginning when Adam blamed Eve and Eve blamed the serpent. It will generally be found that all who are given to some so-called compulsive vice will generally seek out the companionship of those who will never blame them, but rather excuse them; that is, a kind of a confraternity of "innocent babes" is formed by which they insulate themselves from any "moral corruption."

The second effect of the compulsion is the feeling of being divided and torn. It is as if one said, "My name is Legion." The person under compulsion feels very much like the hand when a burning coal is placed upon it; there is no true affinity between the nature of the hand and the nature of a burning coal. This attempt to merge or unite both creates pain. In like manner, it is not the nature of a body to be no longer master of its own fate and destiny. Something is in the mind which is alien to it. Like Macbeth, it asks:

Why do I yield to that suggestion
Whose horrid image doth unfix my hair
And make my seated heart knock at my ribs,
Against the use of nature?

The burning sensation inside of the human psyche means that there is something there which ought not to be there. There is going on inside the one under compulsion something of the struggle of two earthen pots swimming upon the water with the motto: "If we knock together, we sink together." There seems to be a knocking going on in the soul with the prospect of destruction.

A third note of compulsion, and one which closely follows the sensation of duality, is the realization that one cannot be under compulsion except through something other than the ego. That is why a compulsive drinker will say, "I am not to blame! I am under compulsion." No one has better described compulsion than Helmut Thielicke: "I belong to the demonic power, not simply in the sense of belonging to an alien master against my own will. Rather, I belong to that power in the sense that I belong to myself. That is to say, I cannot plead that it simply has control over me and that because of this coercion I incur no responsibility. No, this demonic bondage exists only as I belong to myself, to my ambition, to my selfassertiveness, my passions. The devil lives in the medium of my love of self. I do not love the devil by name, rather I love myself by name and precisely in doing this I deliver myself over to him. Even though I am here dealing with myself, it nevertheless becomes clear that in the very act of doing this, I am dealing with another, simply because I cannot break the bond in which I am held, and am, so to speak, forcibly bound to myself. I see a powerful spell hovering over this bondage."

Goethe's magician's apprentice said, "Those spirits I conjured up, now I can't get rid of them," which is a fairly good description of one under compulsion. But the case is not hopeless. Because there seems to be a power that is overwhelming one who is under compulsion, it follows that only another power is able to master it. In the last analysis, no love is ever driven out; it is only conquered by another love. One cannot overcome a love of alcohol until he finds some other love which is more compelling. One alcoholic told me that nothing and no person ever was able to convince him of the harm he was doing until he saw how it was ruining his wife. It was the love of the wife which eventually drove out the love of alcohol. The deepest mystery, therefore, appears in this final conflict of man's spirit with God's Spirit, and it is only the power of the latter which can drive out and conquer the temporary holder of man's bondage.

† 7 †

Teenagers

The term "teenagers" is not a particularly exact way to describe youth, because the span between thirteen and nineteen is too great. By seventeen generally the character of most youths is formed. A very well-known biographer of Napoleon stated that at fifteen "he was already formed; true, life had something to add to it, but all the defects and good qualities were there in his fifteenth year." Mussolini, fighting with his classmates when he was fifteen, had manifested the same characteristics that he manifested later on. He himself wrote, "I was then formed. I fear that the influences I underwent then were decisive."

If one puts garbage into the stomachs of children, it will be easy to forecast their health; if moral garbage is put into the minds of children, it is easy to predict how these ideas will become acts.

At a United Nations Congress on the prevention of crime, it was strange that no one spoke out more strongly against all pornographic horror publications and immoral literature than L. N. Smirnov of the Soviet Union. He dealt with those who contend that to restrain immoral literature is to curtail freedom saying, "talking about human rights in connection with putting this degrading matter before juveniles, is like the devil quoting the Bible."

This does not mean that youth already bent in the direction of evil cannot become virtuous, for with the grace of God, nothing is impossible. But our present situation rather suggests that youth becomes acquainted with the knowledge of good and evil at too precocious an age. On the morning of an important battle, Napoleon took away from his tent a portrait of his son, the King of Rome. As the bitter struggle was about to begin, he ordered it removed, saying, "It is too soon for him to see a battlefield."

Youth presently is handicapped inasmuch as the major direction of their lives is in the hands of sociologists and psychologists, neither of whom have in their scientific equipment what Dr. Alexis Carrel says are the two essential conditions for developing character: isolation and discipline. Both of these come under the domain of religion and morality. As long as youths travel in herds with their eyes fixed on a one-octave banjo player, they are incapable of reconstructing themselves. As Dr. Carrel put it: "A mode of life which imposes on everyone a constant effort, a psychological and moral discipline and privation, is necessary. An ascetic and mystical minority would rapidly acquire an irresistible power over the self-indulgent and spineless majority." He goes on to say that without this moral self-denial, the intelligence itself becomes anemic. The problem then is not what to do with teenagers; it is who will train them in the Ten Commandments and morality before they are sixteen and seventeen.

Every adult forgets that he was once a teenager. One wonders how many, if they thought about it, would like to return again to that turbulent, juvenile period. Teenage is like death; you cannot thoroughly understand it until you have passed through it. It is an age where one is torn between the desire to express one's own individuality, and yet to be identical with everyone in the group. That is why teenagers dress alike, talk alike, love the same music and the same dances. They are "in" the sheepfold at the moment that they say they are shepherds.

Never again in life will there be such a tension between freedom to express oneself and readiness to be a grape in the wine
vat of teenage-icity.

From another point of view, teenage is a "change of life," a
climactic period in which the biological drives which die later
are now born with a tumultuous physiological and mental
backwash. As the brain is affected by the withdrawal of vital
forces later on in life, so in youth there comes another kind of
hot flash—the alleys and gateways of the body open themselves to the unpredictable and the bizarre.

Teenagers are not the same in each period of history. They,
therefore, must not be judged solely by standards foreign to
their way of life. Neither must one see in them nothing but
guitars, long hair, bony knees and studied unkemptness. As
there are pearls in oysters, so there are treasures in their seeming darkness.

The teenager is right, to some extent, in acting the way he
does. He would go mad in this world if he did not react against
it by doing mad things; he would be frustrated and neurotic if he
accepted the values of a modern civilization which his parents
hold so dear—such as the value that life is for making money.
Teenagers like money, but do not want to make it the main goal
of life. Furthermore, though they have never analyzed it, they
cannot see any righteousness in a system in which six percent
of the population of the world controls forty-six percent of the
world's wealth. They may not know how to equalize it, but
they know that treating our affluent civilization as an island in
the ocean of the world's poverty and misery does not make
sense.

Teenagers never sat down and figured out the modern
stupidities, just as they may never have analyzed the complexity of reasons behind the polluted air of cities, but they know it
is there—they can smell it. They are right in their protests, but
they have no reforms; their protests are immediate, emotional
and without program. Revolutionists, they are, but not like the
old Bolshevik revolutionists who knew what they would set
fire to and what they would build on its ruins. They are pro-
testers without programs, reformers without policy, engines

without flywheels, full of resentment against an older generation which gave them ships but no ports.

The teenagers protest not only against the social and political
injustices, but in a certain sense against the religious world as
well. Religion generally does not touch them. In some instances
this is due to their own want of morals which thrive in the dark
and shrink from the light of betterment. But in some cases, is it
not because those in religion give more precepts than they do
examples? If religion gives a code, youth wants to see the code
lived out in the one who gives it. One cannot throw a book at
teenagers. They see too often disproportion between the nobility of what religion teaches and the mediocrity of the lives of
the teachers; so they excuse themselves from becoming
involved.

Most teenagers who have gone to extremes in their confused
and frustrated lives are little Augustines. Augustine wrote
about his teenage excesses in his *Confessions*. He did everything the worst of teenagers ever did; he did more of it and
more intensely. How did he survive and become so great?
First, because he did a lot of reflecting. Most teenagers do not
think; they just conform and imitate. Augustine advised teenagers to think for themselves, asking such questions as: "Why
do you feel sad when you get violent either physically or eroti-
cally? Why do you squeal and stomp and shriek when you are
with others like yourself, but not when you hear the same
music alone? Why do you feel detribalized when you get outside the herd? Why do you dress like everybody else? Why do
you want liberty without ever thinking whether it means doing
what you *please* or what you *ought*? Can you get out of this
sadness and moroseness by yourself? How high can you lift
yourself by the lobes of your ear? Do you need outside help?"
These reflections were the beginning of Augustine's greatness.
Next he began to love—to love the neighbor, the poor person,
the beggar, the sick boy, the unloved.

No one will ever convince teenagers by argument that they
should know God and their souls. But let them go out and love
the poor, the great unwashed, the sick, and they will find both
God and their souls.

Teenage Personality

What makes a teenager is the emergence of personality. Up until teenage, a youngster is part of a family, readily cooperating with its group actions and submitting to its authority. But, as soon as he becomes a teenager, there is a consciousness of his own ego, a deepening sense of personal responsibility and his differentiation from the family.

This sprouting of personality manifests itself in a trivial way, such as wearing identification, sporting loud socks, making loud noise to draw attention to himself. He will hardly speak in the family, though he will be on the phone for hours giving his ideas to fellow teenagers. Girls no longer play with boys; they curl up with novels and romances and movie magazines. The boy begins to carry a comb, scribbles initials of a girl on the desk, presses his tie, while the pimple on the end of the nose becomes a tremendous worry, particularly on the eve of a dance.

The adolescent is at his best in school and at his worst at home, because he is on his own in school. He seldom talks to "the old man" because "he does not understand." He is peevish with his mother because she does not treat him like a man. "She thinks I'm a kid." The family becomes like an armed camp. The boy hates his sister but not the sisters of other boys.

But even a teenager is a contradiction. He wants to be himself, yet he refuses to be different from others. He asserts his own freedom yet surrenders it to a group. Completely given to imitation, his clothes, attitudes, moods and music are like those of his age group. Ridicule he cannot stand, and this drives him more and more into the destruction of his personality by merging it with an anonymous group. His extreme sensitivity reduces him to the size of an ant in a kind of a composite ant hill.

A survey of high school students revealed that thirty-eight percent considered that the greatest fault of any high school student was not to be one of the group, or to be considered an oddball. Therefore, some of the most favorite expressions of teenagers are: "Aw gee, Ma, none of the other kids are wearing one of those." "Oh, gee, Pa, everybody would make fun of me." "Oh, gee, Ma, the other kids get seventy-eight dollars a week spending money."

The ego and personality which should develop is now lost in the impersonal mass of teenagers. This loss of personality at the very time personality should emerge, does not augur well for the future of democracy. This conformism, imitation, plagiarism, makes it impossible for democracy in a future age to have leaders. Only eighteen percent of high school students admitted that they dared to be any different from the group. But when everybody thinks alike, there is no thought.

If there is any encouragement that parents should give to children when their personalities begin to emerge, it should be "Be yourself." Imitation is actually a desire for authority, but the authority is never defined. It always remains an anonymous authority. It is these same youths who will completely lose themselves in an anonymous authority who will complain against accepting the authority of Christ.

Why Teenagers Rebel

The mood today is to give up on teenagers. Yet who does not know delinquents who became leaders in their community? The Gospels record an instance of this when Judas betrayed Our Blessed Lord and delivered Him over to the soldiers. There was much shouting that midnight in the Garden of Gethsemane, as He was being led away to the house of Caiphas. The excitement awakened a young man who impulsively ran out to see the excitement; the only thing that he had around him was a bed sheet. When he caught up with the officers who had just crossed over the Brook of Kedron, he saw that Our Lord was the prisoner. He began following Him, not just the crowd. Then he remonstrated with the officers who were arresting Him, probably telling them that it was unjust on their part.

The officer, already annoyed by what Peter had done by hacking off the ear of the servant of the high priest, and by the boy's too obvious sympathy for Our Lord, tried to arrest him. Being a teenager, he was much more agile than the police; he slipped out of his linen sheet and ran naked into the darkness.

Later on, this impulsive teenager is found in the company of Paul and Barnabas on their missionary journey. As long as they stayed on the blue waters of the sea and visited Cyprus, this teenager was an ardent missionary, but when Paul and Barnabas started going inland among robbers and mountain streams and dangers, this young man found the going too rough, and his missionary zeal ran out. He ran well at first, but he could not keep up the pace. Paul told him to go back to his mother in Jerusalem; but later on, the teenager comes through. Paul speaks of him as being a fellow worker and as being very profitable to him in the ministry. It must be remembered that this teenager who stumbled through life, found literary immortality, for he wrote the Second Gospel. His name was Mark.

Three youths once were expelled from their schools. One because he was always drawing pictures in geography class, the other because he was constantly fighting during recreation, and the third because he kept revolutionary literature under the mattress. No one today remembers the valedictorians or the bright boys of those classes, but there is no one in the world who does not know the first boy who was Hitler; the second, who was Mussolini; and the third, who was Stalin. How their teachers must have wished that they had been more patient!

Youth has higher aspirations than adults generally suspect, but adults do not challenge these aspirations, nor lead them to the heights. The young people today have a spirit of sacrifice and a readiness for surrender which has been untapped.

The Communists, the Nazis and the Fascists in the last generation knew how to appeal to the sacrificial spirit in youth. Youth is sick and tired of a milk and water liberalism which calls for no self-denial. But the elders fail to awaken that latent spirit.

Can an alcoholic father ever convince his teenage son to be temperate? Can a mother who has been divorced three times ever tell her teenage daughter that she must always be true to her word? Why not? Because reverence for a precept depends on reverence for the one who gives the precept. A teenager

instinctively knows that if parents do not recognize any authority over him, then by what right do the parents command?

Teenagers do not ever state this clearly: they do not even
know the instinctive reason why they rebel against their parents; but like little cogs, they rebel against the big cogs who
refuse to do as they should.

The fourth commandment of God which is: Honor thy father
and thy mother, is the link between the first three, which relate
to our duties to God, and the last six, which relate to our duties
as neighbors. From this commandment follows this truth: Parents who honor God always find it easy to train the children to
honor them, the parents; children who honor parents always
find it easy to honor the Heavenly Father. Juvenile delinquency
will diminish when parents learn that God is not a swear word.

Hard to Be a Teenager

It is hard to be a teenager. I wonder how many adults would
like to go through all the crises of adolescence again. George
Bernard Shaw said that it was a pity that youth was wasted on
the young. Jerome K. Jerome said to a woman who was
thirty-nine, "I think it is a beautiful age—young enough not
have lost the joy of youth, old enough to have learned sympathy." Euripides, the pre-Christian Greek dramatist, praised
youth as being the "best time to be rich and the best time to be
poor." Shakespeare called teenage the "salad days when I was
green in judgment." An English proverb takes another point of
view: "Those who would be young when they are old, must be
old when they are young."

To be a teenager is hard for many reason. In our contemporary society, youth is interested in politics, social affairs, slum
clearance and racial justice. Because the young see things
either as black or white, their love of justice comes out nega-
tively as a protest against a society which they believe tolerates
these abuses. While this is all well and good in youth, a concern for the distressed entails no obvious deprivation, no spirit
of poverty in cutting down their spending money. In fact, the
young have the same tensions as religion often does when it
fails to share its wealth with the poor.

Enduring no social hardships, they, too, pontificate against social abuses from ivory towers or from dens laden with a hundred discs. One finds this particularly in the "Great Unwashed" who protest against the society in which they live and yet in their workless days, depend on money sent to them by parents who could not afford to do so unless they lived in the society against which their "hippie" children rebel.

Adults see this inconsistency between blaming and helping much more clearly; that is why lucrative positions in life are often surrendered in order to serve the poor. Five doctors and professors in one medical school in the United States have practically given up their practice in order to serve in a clinic. Grown-ups clearly see that they must not protest unless they can reform, and they cannot reform unless their protest turns into some surrender of their possessions.

But does not even the protest of youth offer hope? Will not their present yearning for social betterment in the midst of their affluence later on turn to an abandonment of affluence in order to remake society? Certainly no previous generation of young Americans ever felt so keenly the need of becoming Good Samaritans to the peoples of rat-infested ghettos.

Did the present Jet Set ever have the same sense of responsibility to the poor in their youth, as the youths do today? They were probably devoid of a passion for social justice. The teenager of today will probably never lose his desire to make a better world; he will just sharpen it and work more cooperatively with all segments of society.

A second reason why it is hard to be a teenager is that his parents are now living in a world that is radically different from that of their youth when there were no atomic bombs, flights to the moon, or unravelings of the border line between chemistry and life. For them to say to their children, "In my day . . . " is nonsense. That day is gone forever. On the other hand, neither the parents nor the children have any idea of the kind of world we will be living in twenty years from now. Both the old and the young are facing the world of the future as they would a city in Europe which they have never before visited.

How is it possible to give directions or find one's way when there are no signposts? If children accuse parents of being "behind the times," parents might well retort that children are "behind the times" every year they live. Like the automatic rabbit in the dog race, technical progress always keeps ahead of them. For that reason, there has to be some guidance which is neither of the past nor of the future. The one thing is the teachings of the Gospel, which did not suit the times. The refrain rings out: "It has been said to you of old." Then comes, "But I say to you . . . Heaven and earth may pass away, but My Word will not pass away." Old and young can both drink of this fountain and become young again. Only something that does not suit the times can save the times.

Teenage Sensitiveness

It is too bad that teenagers cannot write good autobiographies so that their keen sensitiveness would be revealed. But this is asking too much, since such writing requires standing off and viewing oneself from a distance and the perspective of time. Furthermore, as one ages one develops more humility and with it the ability to laugh at one's mistakes. We see others long before we see ourselves. In *The Scapegoat*, Daphne du Maurier wrote, "Someone jolted my elbow as I drank and said, 'Pardon me, please,' and as I moved to give him space, he turned and stared at me and I at him. I realized with a strange sense of shock and fear and nausea all combined that his face and voice were known to me too well. I was looking at myself."

Teenagers often go through a humiliation bordering on crucifixion through sensitiveness. What a tragedy is a pimple on the face, a skirt that is too long, a coat that is too short, the father who comes to the school with greasy overalls—overalls are all right, but not greasy ones—the mother who has an accent, the reprimand before the class, the indifferent look of a fellow student and, above all, the dread of being classified into the trinity of outcasts: as a "crumb, dumb or bum."

Standards are built into the life of teenagers, and conformism is rigid. An elephant apart from the herd is not as panic-stricken as one who dresses well when others do not, or who refuses to smoke pot when others do. The dread of not being like others makes them fearful of using their own judgment, of listening to an inner voice or of ever making a self-appraisal apart from the mob. There is a market price that is fixed, and every teenager must sell himself at that figure.

But, at the same time, the teenager has another drive which is the opposite of conformism. It is a desire to be an emerging personality, not a rubber stamp. His conformism is, in part aided by a rebellion against being molded by elders, but his emerging individuality makes him sometimes wish he could be different. Teenagers are like ants who want to live in the swarm of the anthill, and at the same time, they would like to be the ant who is brave enough to go to a picnic alone.

This drive to be an individual is expressed in their poetry and songs which stress "I want to be me." The truth is, there is one sense in which the self most discovers itself and that is: *in serving and loving others*. When does a teenager become more conscious of his personality than after he has forgotten it by volunteering in a hospital, teaching dropouts, cleaning up slums and mowing the old widow's lawn? When his heart says, "I want to be for others," that is the moment when his sense of dignity and worth is at its peak.

The happy teenager is the one who balances this tendency to be absorbed in the lives of others, with the opposite drive to emerge as a unique person. This happens when teenagers are open to insights which persons other than their peers may give them about themselves.

Paul Nathanson, one father, tells of an experience he had in comparing his son's qualities with his own. Ten attributes or qualities were set down as the standard. Each agreed to mark those qualities in which he believed himself superior. In the final tally, the son believed himself superior to the father in seven attributes, below him in only one, and equal in the other two. The father was more generous to the son, but what resulted was a greater self-knowledge of each and a greater confidence in one another.

Generally, this mutual "give and take" is lacking. A teenager rarely gets any correction after childhood. If a parent does give it, the answer invariably is, "But look what you do! You are not so faultless," as if the fault in another canceled out the fault in self. Elders, too, may be to blame by concentrating on the fault: "Look what you have done now," instead of inspiring confidence by saying, "What can we do now?"

The reconciliation of this contradiction in teenagers, to surrender oneself to the mob as a drop of water in a glass of wine, and to want "to be me" with no regard for others, is that Divine injunction" "Love your neighbor as yourself." "As yourself" implies a degree of self-love, self-respect, but instead of crawling inside a shell of egotism, one is to direct this personality outward, serving humanity, and especially the poor. No one appreciates a final spiritual liberation so much as the one who has long been imprisoned in defeat and despair, and then discovers his true freedom. It is egotism that spoils us. Few indeed ever reach that humility which makes for greatness as the preacher who, when congratulated on his sermon by a gushing friend who said, "you were magnificient," answered, "The devil already told me."

Help for Teenagers

Anyone who has been privileged to read the diaries of teenagers will discover their tortures inadequately expressed, but poignantly felt. One writes, "I'm more and more bored with myself, and I don't talk as much as I used to. Girls don't understand me. I wish I could see Marie, the one I met last summer. She is the only one who would ever listen to what I say." From another teenager's diary, "Mom's too busy and she never listens. Dad says I will never amount to anything. I wish I knew what to do with myself. I look in the mirror and wonder, what is me? I could almost cry. . . . Mary said that no man would ever marry her with her bad teeth and pimples."

These are really tragic deliverances and these troubled souls are looking for ways out of these dilemmas. Perhaps a few suggestions would help.

1. Note the difference between what happens to you and the way you react to what happens. A little pimple appears on the nose and you go into a tailspin. Your emotions are running away with your reason. The emotional response must always be in proportion to that which prompted it, but never in excess of it. If a pimple gets you down now, think of what business routine will do to you in ten years. You will call it the "rat

race." Every night, give yourself a few moments of quiet and force petty worries out of your mind. As a wise man wrote:

On a branch that swings
Sits a bird that sings
Knowing it has wings.

2. Study those in school who are the most popular and those who are the most unpopular. Then ask yourself why? You will discover that the popular boy or girl is the one who is pleasant to everyone, who gives a helping hand to others and who never talks about himself. The unpopular youth is the one who high-hats almost everyone except his few friends, is sarcastic, and laughs at others' mistakes. If you want to be loved, stop loving yourself, or feeling sorry for yourself. When you get older you will find that even your sickness will last less long if you are surrounded by the thoughtfulness and love of others. Dr. Karl Menninger, the famous psychiatrist, once wrote, "You cure by atmosphere, by attitude, by sympathetic understanding on the part of everyone in the hospital." Most young people become unpopular by trying to be popular. Popularity is a bridesmaid, not a bride; it is a by-product of considerateness of others. Narcissus loved himself and Echo loved Narcissus. But he kept staring at his own image in the pool and thus could find no time for her. Echo left weeping. Popularity is a feedback from self-forgetfulness.

3. Do not fall in love with an experience, but only with a person. This is difficult during teenage, because girls like boys and boys like girls. They enjoy the contrast of masculinity and femininity. Love is really love only when the object is a person. The trick is to distinguish between the person and the experience of feeling in love which the other engenders. Experiences are replaceable, but persons are not. No one can take the place of your father or your mother. You will often find that what makes you flip is a look, a kind word, a bit of attention or the touch of a hand. Never confuse the electric wire which gives you the shock with the manager of the Electric Light Company.

4. Grow up as quickly as you can, so that you do not fall in

love either with masculinity or femininity. You have often heard about pinup girls. These pictures are sold by the hundreds of thousands, and they are all of the same girls. There is a world of difference between loving the general and loving the particular. One can love a garden, but few want a garden in the house as a life companion. Many love humanity, as did Rousseau, but he abandoned each of his children after birth. Love in the abstract is a world apart from love in the concrete. On the other hand, neither is falling in love with a fraction the same as loving a person. Many a man falls in love with a dimple and makes the mistake of marrying the whole woman. This does not mean that one should become so desperate that the boy takes everything he can get, and the girl takes anything she can get.

5. There are two kinds of love: need love and gift love. Need love is something every heart possesses. Just as the eye needs light, the ear sound and the stomach food, so every heart needs love. But gift love is that which we bestow even when it is not needed. If you saw a little child on the street and in danger of traffic, your gift love would urge you to save the life of the child. Gift love does not help us directly; it helps others. Gift love makes us happier than being satisfied with need love. If you are ever generous enough to understand gift love, then you can understand why God came down into the muck and dirt of human life to teach us love—the love that goes on loving even when it is not returned.

Teenagers and Happiness

A teenager develops like an icicle. When the icicle begins to form, its color is determined by the drops of water which enter into its formation. If the water is clean, the icicle is clear and transparent; if the water is dirty, the icicle does not glow. So with a teenager. Every thought, pure or foul in his or her mind, every act of kindness or hate becomes a part of character. Teenagers often wonder why their elders can foretell what kind of men or women they will make. The reason is that one need not throw a log into a stream to find which way the current is flowing: a straw will do just as well.

Every teenager wants to be happy, although when you listen to their songs, so full of a yearning for death, one sometimes wonders. But this sadness is because they are already spoiled and disillusioned. Yet before they allow the worm of evil to eat the apple of their lives, they really want to be happy. That is what the Beatitudes of Our Lord were about: eight rules for being happy, each one beginning with, "Happy are they . . ." There are two ways to be happy though a teenager:

1. Do not monkey with the carburetor of your car. When you buy a car, a set of directions is given by the manufacturer, e.g., when to grease it, oil it, etc. These instructions were never meant to cramp your style or destroy your freedom. Rather, like the advice of any professional, they are designed to enable you to get the maximum of pleasure out of the machine. The carburetor which controls the flow of gas into the cylinders is very delicate and finely adjusted; so you are told, "Do not monkey with the carburetor."

Your conscience is like the carburetor. God put into your conscience certain directions for leading a happy life, but if you heed others who tell you to follow them instead of your conscience, you will feel an inner unhappiness like the spitting of the motor if you fool with the carburetor. If you fail to heed these warnings, you may eventually get into a state where you will say, "Oh! There isn't any manufacturer of an automobile; these so-called directions are just man-made taboos. I want to be free from restraints." You will be! But you will be "free" like a pendulum freed from the clock—useless and unable to swing in the rhythmic joy of order and inner peace. Go on rebelling against the inner voice which is the voice of God, and you will feel frustrated, miserable, unhappy, and wish you were dead!

God has written a wonderful symphony for life, well-scored and easy to follow if we study the music. You will make a life full of harmony and will live in peace with the other musicians who are your fellow citizens, if you but heed the notes.

2. "Get out of your teenage nest as fast as you can." Teenage is really only a small bridge connecting childhood with maturity. It is a transition period, not a career. You happen to be living in a country which has the longest adolescence period of any in the world. One is not a teenager until nineteen; one is

a teenager as long as he fails to mature into an acceptance of responsibilities.

All those who are destined for greatness get out of the period of immaturity as soon as possible. Meet the challenge in the world around about you. Be young men! Be young women! Because the word "teen" is still in nine*teen* it does not mean that you have to wait that long to realize that you are not here to have the world serve you, but for you to serve the world. In this adventure into responsibility, Heaven will help you. In the book of Deuteronomy, we read that as the eagles stir in the nests of the young and hover over them, so God stirs and hovers over us. God's loving compulsion is aimed at effort. He "stirs up the warm nest of teenagers' irresponsibility" by the pricking of conscience, by the inner voice of the Spirit and sometimes by trial—anything to make us grow up. Otherwise, we would stiffen in juvenile habits, becoming mental dwarfs. The stirring of the nest is actually the sign of the closer approach of the Father guiding our lives. If we lay ourselves in God's ways—after having tried ourselves—He will see that no harm comes to us. Out of the nest, out of the cradle!

Teenage Respect

Some parents complain that their teenage children never obey them; other parents deny that they have any difficulties in this area. Why the difference?

The difference is not always in the children, as is too often assumed; it may lie in the parents. The rebellion against the authority of the elders is not always because teenagers are opposed to authority, but rather because of those who administer authority. St. Thomas Aquinas, one of the greatest philosophers who ever lived, gave this rule in Latin which is worth quoting: *"Ex reverentia praecipientis procedere debet reverentia praecepti."* (The respect that one has for a rule flows from the respect that one has for the one who gives it).

When it comes to music, for example, teenagers are very willing to accept the authority of a band leader, because they feel he knows his subject and is qualified to speak on it. The teenage boy will accept the authority of a well-known baseball player on the subject of sports, because his accomplishments are worthy of respect in that field. It was said of the soldiers of Napoleon that if anyone had cut out their hearts, they would have seen his image engraved thereon—so much did they respect his ability as a soldier.

Little boys never have any difficulty in accepting the authority of their parents. "My daddy told me" is their final word on any subject. Later on, when the little boy becomes a teenager, there is not that same spontaneous acceptance of parental authority; there must be added another reason for parental respect, and that is the moral worth of the one who gives it. Where there is love, because of the nobility of the character of the parents, there is obedience. Our Blessed Lord based obedience to His Commandments upon love: "If you love Me, you will keep My Commandments." Before He gave Peter the authority to rule over His lambs and sheep, He asked him three times, "Do you love Me?" Once there was a love admitted for Christ on the basis of His conquest over evil, then there would be no question whatever of obedience to His commands.

When a teacher lacks that moral and intellectual value which commands respect, disobedience results. The rise of juvenile delinquency is in direct proportion to the decline of moral values among the parents. If the parents of teenagers are intemperate, given to alcoholism, infidelity, quarreling and fighting, what can be expected of the children? If parents have made second marriages, with first spouses still living, it is impossible for these parents to say to their children, "You must keep your word and never break it"; the children know they have already broken a word concerning loving unto death. It will not do for alcoholic parents to say, "You must not drink," if the children have seen either of the parents drunk.

On the contrary, when parents set a worthy example for their children, obedience is not rendered by the children because of a fear of punishment, but rather because they would not hurt those whom they love. The commandment of God: "Thou shalt honor thy father and thy mother," implies honor in the parents. Honor is a recognition of the excellence of someone.

It would be quite wrong always to blame the children for

failure to honor their parents. Honor and dishonor, love and aversion, respect and disgust are born in them, according to what they see in the parents. Sometimes it may be the duty of teenagers to educate their parents. To parents who have not given good example, the teenagers must be given their counsel: The last generation has failed you; but you must not fail the next generation.

Teenage Love

A sixteen-year-old boy who was "madly in love," begged his parents to invite the parents of his girl friend to the house. When told that it might not be wise to plunge too quickly into marriage, he answered his parents, "Yes, but you do not know what love really is." This kind of argument is given generally by two classes of people—teenagers in love and enthusiasts of cubistic art: "You don't understand it." Instead of proving what they know, they argue that you are unknowing. The trick is not so much to show that they are omniscient, but rather that others are nescient. Perhaps teenagers might be spared dangerous plunges into unhappiness, did they know a "few facts of life." Here are some questions they might ask themselves to sharpen their understanding.

1. "Am I in love with a person, or am I in love with love?" There are certain experiences which are absolutely new to youth. Because they are associated with the glands, the blood cells and generally with what are called passions, they force themselves upon youth with a violence and intensity which are apt to destroy reason and judgment. When a man is being chased by a wild bull in the field, it is hardly the moment to decide whether he will make his money by being a banker or labor leader. Similarly, a youth who is enjoying an initial experience might inquire if he loves what another person excites in him, or whether he loves the person.

2. "Do I realize that sex is replaceable, but love is not?" The mere enjoyment of passion as such can be indifferent to persons in its grip, but love can never be indifferent. No one can ever take the place of a mother, a father or a best friend.

When they are gone, the niches remain empty for the rest of life. But the mere enjoyment of food can be experienced with a great variety of dishes. It is easy for youth to feel that the first one who ever aroused a feeling of love is the only love that is possible. One might just as well drink milk out of a bottle all his life, because the satisfaction of taste first came through a bottle. Some indeed do retain this devotion to a bottle; it corresponds with "going steady" with the first person who ever excited a gland. But if a person is loved, rather than the emotion, then that person is loved without change or alteration *"until death do us part!"*

3. "Do I think that the passion and the romantic feeling I have for a 'steady' now will endure with ever-increasing depth and intensity?" If this be true, why don't the parents of teenagers act toward one another like teenagers act toward one another? It is doubtful that the teenager has a power which no adult ever possessed. But the teenager assumes that passion is something that will enrich the organism through life, will fill it with endless transports, ever more intense and gratifying. Hunger for food is to some extent like the hunger for love. Why are there more ulcers at forty than at fourteen? Why do men, when they get old, give up fried foods? Something happened to the hunger; something like that happens to all hungers, with the possible exception of avarice. This does not mean that love decreases as time goes on; but it does mean that the biological and erotic accompaniment of love decreases. Therefore, one has to make sure that it is a person and not a "thrill" that one loves.

4. "If I fall in love with an 'ideal,' will I marry a 'fact'?" The ideal has the nature of the infinite about it; because it is a dream, it surrounds itself with the dimension of eternity and unending bliss. Nothing sets a limit to a dream. But in marriage, the ideal begins to be a fact; what was the ideal, becomes "cabined and cribbed and confined." The great luminous desire is now reduced to a concrete image. The fog has lifted.

In other words, every woman promises a man that which God alone can give; every man promises a woman that which God alone can give. They are right in having the ideal; they are wrong in thinking that the other partner can give what heaven reserves for itself alone. The best of human love is only a spark which fell from the great Flame of Love, which is God. Marriage is not an experience in which there is an exchange of mutual egotisms, and in which the bond lasts only as long as the other gives a thrill; rather it is a symbol of a great mystery—the mystery of God Who fell in love with man and took upon Himself a human nature—forever. Marriage representing that eternal union, therefore lasts *"until death do us part."*

† 8 †

The Sacrifice of the Mass

Some things in life are too beautiful to be forgotten. These things may be what men do in this world; they may even be their manner of passing from it. For example, almost every country has instituted a memorial day to recall the supreme sacrifice its patriots have made in defense of country and civilization. Because life was the most precious thing they could give, the living cannot forget their gift. They themselves could not ask for any such memorial, nor could they institute it; that was left to their survivors.

If it is fitting that we have memorial days for those who died to preserve freedom from the oppression of men, it is fitting, too, that there be a memorial for the supreme sacrifice of Christ, Who died to give us freedom from the tyranny of sin. There are many differences, however, between those patriots and Christ. No one of them was born to die; each was born to live and death was for each a brutal interruption. But Our Lord came to die; it was the goal of His life, it was the goal He was seeking. For no other purpose came He into the world than to redeem sinful humanity.

Furthermore, unlike the men who could not make their own memorial, He instituted the precise way in which His death was to be recalled. Since He came to die, this death was the chief thing He wished us to remember. He did not say that men should write a history of it, or even that they should be kind to the poor in memory of Him; He gave them the exact manner in which He wished this sacrifice to be commemorated. The memorial He gave us is called the Mass.

It was instituted the night before he died at what has since then been called the Last Supper. Taking bread into his hands He said: "This is my body, which is to be given for you," that is, the next day on the cross. Then over the chalice of wine, He said: "This is my blood, of the new testament, which is to be shed for many to the remission of sins." He was a priest offering Himself as a victim so that men might never forget that "greater love than this no man hath than that he lay down his life for his friends." And after prefiguring and foreshadowing the way in which He would die the next day for the redemption of the world, He gave the Divine command to His Apostles and to His Church: "Do this for a commemoration of Me." In that Last Supper He looked *forward* to the Cross; in the Mass we *look back* to it.

The Mass is the application and the projection through space and time of the redemptive love of Christ on the Cross. Imagine a radio station sending out messages from all eternity, it is there all the time but we only hear the messages as we begin to tune in. So, too, the sacrifice that was offered on the Cross has an eternal value, but the Mass helps more and more people to "tune in" on its merits and to apply them to themselves.

The Redemption of Our Lord on the Cross was offered once for all, but its actualization has depended upon the unfolding of history. Potentially every human being in the world was redeemed on the cross; the actualization and the application of that redemption depend upon the free cooperation of man in the course of history.

Calvary took up only a moment of time, but being the sacrifice of the Eternal God made man, it was capable of illumining the whole of time in all periods of history. The Mass is the projection in time of the eternal values of Calvary.

Similarly Calvary was only one small place on the earth at the crossroads of Jerusalem, Athens and Rome, but what took place there, the sacrifice of the Omnipotent, can affect man everywhere in all corners of the earth. The Mass plants the cross in a town, in a village, in a mission, in a great cathedral; it draws back the curtains on time and space and makes what happened on Calvary happen there. The cross affected all past history by *anticipation;* all the sacrifices of bullocks, and goats, and sheep, and particularly the sacrifice of the paschal lamb, found their completion on the cross. The cross affected also the *future,* by flowing out through all time, like a mighty waterfall or cascade which makes channels through valleys and plains.

The very fact that all sacrifices practically ceased after the sacrifice of Calvary, meant that Calvary was the perfection and the fulfillment of *all* sacrifices. Even the Jews no longer sacrifice paschal lambs in their synagogues, for the True Paschal Lamb has already been sacrificed.

The sacrifice of the Cross, therefore, is not something that happened more than 1900 years ago, it is something that is still happening. It is not an heirloom or an antique which endures into the present, it is a drama as actual now as then, and so it will remain as long as time and eternity endure.

On the Cross Our Blessed Lord knew how every individual soul in the world would react to His supreme act of love, whether or not they would accept Him or reject Him. We ourselves do not know how we will react until we are confronted with Christ and His Cross, and we see it unrolled on the screen of time. From our point of view, it takes time to see the drama unfolded. But the Mass gives us an intimation; we were not conscious of being present on Calvary on Good Friday, but we are consciously present at the Mass. We can know something of the role we played at Calvary by the way we act at the Mass in the twentieth century, and by the way the Mass helps us to live.

The Mass is not a *new sacrifice* but another *enactment* of the one supreme sacrifice of Calvary. There are two moments in history, one when the sacrifice is expected and the other when the sacrifice is possessed and offered. The first moment is called B.C., the second moment is called A.D.

If the Blessed Mother and St. John at the foot of the Cross had closed their eyes when Our Lord was offering Himself for the sins of the world, the spiritual effects on them would have been no different from those which we may receive as we assist at the Sacrifice of the Mass. But if their eyes were open, there would have been this difference: they would have seen the sacrifice offered in bloodshed with blood pouring from gaping holes in hands and feet and side. In the Mass, we see it performed without bloodshed.

The Mass, therefore, is not a substitute for the Cross, but the merit we gain at the Mass is the same as the merit we would have gained if we had assisted at Calvary.

The reason there is only one sacrifice is that the Priest and the Victim, both on the Cross and in the Mass, are one and the same person. Up until the coming of the Son of God, there were many sacrifices offered for sins. Men felt that they were unfit to exist before the Divine Presence. By taking the life of an animal or by destroying a thing, they vicariously punished and purified themselves. Among all peoples, in addition to the Jews who had the great advantage of Divine revelation, there were therefore, priests who offered victims of sacrifice. Their task was to slay the goat or the sheep, or pour out the wine, or immolate the bull. But when Our Lord came, He became at one and the same time *Priest* and *Victim,* He became both the Offerer and the One Who was offered. No longer were the priest and victims *separate* as they had been before. On the Cross, therefore, He was upright as a Priest; He was prostrate as a Victim because He was offering Himself.

The Priest offers the Mass only as the representative of Christ, hence he does not say, at the moment of consecration, this is the Body and Blood of Christ but "This is My Body" and "This is My Blood"; he is only an instrument of Christ in the same way that a pencil is an instrument of one who writes.

We said that one of the differences between the Cross and the Mass was that in the Mass the sacrifice is offered without bloodshed, whereas on the Cross there were the heart-rending scenes of Crucifixion. A second difference is that on the Cross Our Lord was alone while in the Mass we are with Him. How we are with Him, will be made clear if we examine the Offertory, the Consecration and the Communion.

Offertory

In order to apply the merits of redemption to our souls we must recapitulate in ourselves the death to sin which was brought about on the Cross. Hence, the first act is the offering of ourselves in union with Christ. In the early Church this was done by offering the very same elements which Our Lord Himself offered at the Last Supper; namely, bread and wine. In the early Church the faithful brought bread and wine to the Mass and some of each was used by the priest for the sacrifice. There are some intrinsic reasons why these elements should have been used, even apart from their Divine authorization. First, bread and wine had been the traditional nourishment of most men through history. Bread, as it were, is the very marrow of the earth and wine is as its very blood. The faithful, therefore, in offering that which has given them their physical sustenance and life, are equivalently giving themselves. A second reason is that no two substances in nature better represent unity than do bread and wine. Bread is made from a multiplicity of grains of wheat, wine from a multiplicity of grapes. So the faithful, who are many, combine to make one offering with Christ. A third reason is that few elements in nature better symbolize sacrifice than wheat and grapes. Wheat does not become bread until it has passed through the Calvary of a winter and has been subjected to the tortures of the mill. Grapes do not become wine until they have trodden the Gethsemane of the press. Today, the faithful no longer all bring bread and wine to the Sacrifice of the Mass but they bring the equivalent; that is the reason why the collection is often taken up at what is called the Offertory of the Mass. The material sacrifice which they make for the Mass is still a symbol of their spiritual incorporation in the death of Christ. Though they bring no bread and wine, they bring that which buys bread and wine, and these elements still represent the material of their united sacrifice.

Consecration

We have offered ourselves to God as Our Lord offered Himself to His Heavenly Father. The essence of Christianity is the reproduction of what happened to Our Blessed Lord in the life of every single person in the world. The human nature which He took was the pattern, or model nature, for all of us. As He was crucified, rose again and ascended into glory for the redemption of the world, so every person is to offer his human nature freely to Our Blessed Lord and to die to sin in order to live in grace and glory with Him. The Mass represents the peak of that incorporation into the death and glory of Christ. In the offertory we present ourselves to God under the form of bread and wine.

Now we come to the Consecration, when what is known as Transubstantiation takes place. We are beginning to die to the lower part of ourselves in order to live to Christ. Transubstantiation means that when the words of Consecration are pronounced, the substance of the bread becomes the substance of the Body of Christ, and the substance of the wine becomes the substance of His Blood. It has for its effect a new presence without bloodshed, of the offering of Calvary. In the Mass, there is not another offering, but only another presence of the same offering through the ministry of the priest.

The bread and wine are not consecrated together but separately. First the bread which becomes His Body, then the wine which becomes His Blood. This separate consecration of the bread and wine is a kind of mystical separation of His Body and His Blood, equivalent to the way He died on Calvary.

The consecration of the Mass does not mean that Our Lord dies again, for He never can die again in His own individual human nature, which is now in glory at the right hand of the Father. But He prolongs His death in us. That is one of the reasons that there must always be a servant or server, a member of the Church in attendance when the Mass is said. The Mass is the offering of the living Church and its faithful. It is almost as if at the moment of consecration Our Lord were saying: "I cannot die again in My human nature which is in glory at the right hand of the Father, but Peter, Paul, Mary, James, Ann: you give Me your human nature and I will die again in you." In the Offertory we presented ourselves for sacrifice with Christ; in the Consecration we die with Him. We apply His death to ourselves that we may share His glory. The eternal now breaks in upon the temporal and there is nothing more solemn on the face of the earth than the awe-inspiring moment of consecration. It is not a prayer, it is not a hymn, it is not something said, it is a Divine act which enables us to apply the Cross to ourselves.

Though primarily the words of consecration mean that the Body and Blood of Christ is present on the altar, there is a secondary meaning which concerns ourselves. The priests and the people are also called to make such a total dedication of themselves, by death to sin and lower life, that they can say: "This is my body, this is my blood. I care not if the species or the accidents or the appearances of my life remain, such as my duty in life, my avocations, my employment. Let all these things stay as they are, but what I am before Thee, my intellect, my will, my body, my soul, let all these be so changed that I may be not mine but Thine." Then we realize in the deepest sense, the words of St. Paul to the Galatians: "With Christ I hang upon the cross." We might put it into a prayer, saying: "I give myself to God, here is my body, take it. Here is my blood, take it. Here is my soul, my will, my energy, my strength, my property, my wealth—all that I have. It is Yours. Take it! Consecrate it! Offer it! Offer it with Thyself to the Heavenly Father in order that He, looking down on this great sacrifice, may see only Thee, His Beloved Son, in Whom He is well pleased. Transmute the poor bread of my life into Thy Divine Life; charge the wine of my wasted life with Thy Divine Spirit; unit my broken heart with Thy Heart; change my cross into a crucifix. Let not my abandonment, my sorrow and my bereavement go to waste. Gather up the fragments, and as the drop of water is absorbed by the wine at the Offertory of the Mass, let my life be absorbed in Thine; let my little cross be entwined with Thy great Cross so that I may purchase the joys of everlasting happiness in union with Thee."

The Communion

In the Offertory, we are like lambs being led to the slaughter. In the Consecration, we are the lambs who are slaughtered in the lower part of our sinful selves. In the Communion, we find that we have not died at all but that we have come to life.

In order to understand by opposites what takes place in Holy Communion, consider the nature of a totalitarianism such as Communism. In such a philosophy of life, every person must surrender himself totally and completely, body and soul, mind and will, action and life, to a human dictator. In Christianity there is also a total surrender; we give ourselves complete and entirely to God through His Divine Son, Jesus Christ.

But here comes the great difference. In Communism those who deliver themselves over to the state are surrendering to materialism, for they are denying God and the soul. When one gives oneself up to that which is material, one becomes possessed by it, as a drowning man becomes possessed by the materiality of fire, and a suffocated man becomes possessed by the materiality of earth. Communism can never enrich or exalt the souls of its followers.

But when there is a dedication to God, and when our death is to the lower part of ourselves as it is in the Consecration of the Mass, then we get back our souls ennobled and enriched. We begin at last to be free, glorified, divinized, exalted. We find that, after all, our death was no more permanent in the Consecration than was the death of Christ on Calvary, for in Holy Communion we surrender our humanity and we receive Divinity. We give up time and we get eternity, we give up our sin and we receive grace, we surrender our self-will and receive the omnipotence of Divine will. We give up petty loves and receive the Flame of Love, we give up our nothingness and we receive all. For Christ has said: "He . . . who loses his life for my sake . . . will save it."

There is another life above the life of the body; namely, the life of the soul. Just as the life of the body is the soul, so, too, the life of the soul is God. This Divine life we receive in Communion. If the sunlight and moisture and the chemicals of the earth could speak they would say to the plants: "Unless you eat me you shall not have life in you;" if the plants and the herbs of the field could speak, they would say to the animals: "Unless you eat me you shall not have life in you;" if the animals and plants and the chemicals of the universe could speak they would say to man: "Unless you eat me you shall not have life in you." So, too, the Son of God says to us that unless we receive of Him we shall not have Divine life in us. The law of transformation holds sway, the lower is transformed into the higher; chemicals into plants, plants into animals, animals into man and man into God without, however, man ever losing his personal identity. Hence the word that is used for Communion is "to receive" Our Lord, for literally we do receive the Divine life, more significantly than a babe receives human life as it is nursed by the mother, for in this latter case, the human is being nourished by the human, but in Communion the human receives Divine life from God. But like all words, even this one has some imperfection for in communion it is not so much we who receive Christ as Christ who receives us, incorporating us into Himself.

We know we do not deserve this. All love really feels itself unworthy. The lover is always on his knees, the beloved always on a pedestal. Hence before receiving Communion we repeat with the priest: "O, Lord, I am not worthy." It is as if we were holding ourselves back, conscious of the fact that we are unworthy of the Divine gift.

It is to be noted that there is no such thing as Communion without a sacrifice. Just as we cannot have the natural communion of eating, unless vegetables have been torn up from their roots and subjected to fire, and animals have been subjected to the knife and slain, and then submitted to purgation, so neither can we have Communion with Christ unless there is first a death. That is why the Mass is not just a Communion service; it is a sacrifice which ends in Communion. Communion is the consequence of Calvary; we live by what we slay. Our bodies live by the slaying of the beasts of the field and the plants of the garden; we draw life from their crucifixion; we slay them not to destroy but to have life more abundantly. We immolate them for the sake of communion.

By a beautiful paradox of Divine love, God makes His Cross

† 9 †

A Divine Sense of Humor

No one can ever understand the sacraments unless he has what might be called a "divine sense of humor." A person is said to have a sense of humor if he can "see through" things; one lacks a sense of humor if he cannot "see through" things. No one has ever laughed at a pun who did not see in the one word a twofold meaning. To materialists this world is opaque like a curtain; nothing can be seen through it. A mountain is just a mountain, a sunset just a sunset; but to poets, artists, and saints, the world is transparent like a window pane—it tells of something beyond; for example, a mountain tells of the Power of God, the sunset of His Beauty, and the snowflake of His Purity.

When the Lord Incarnate walked this earth, He brought to it what might be called a "divine sense of humor." There is only one thing that He took seriously, and that was the soul. He said: "What exchange shall a man give for his soul?" Everything else was a telltale of something else. Sheep and goats, wine bottles and patches on clothing, camels and eyes of needles, the lightning flash and the red of the sunset sky, the fisherman's nets and Caesar's coin, chalices and rich men's gates—all of these were turned into parables and made to tell the story of the Kingdom of God.

Our Lord had a divine sense of humor, because He revealed that the universe was sacramental. A sacrament, in a very broad sense of the term, combines two elements: one visible, the other invisible—one that can be seen, or tasted, or touched, or heard; the other unseen to the eyes of the flesh. There is, however, some kind of relation or significance between the two. A spoken word is a kind of sacrament, because there is something material or audible about; there is also something spiritual about it, namely, its meaning. A horse can hear a funny story just as well as a man. It is conceivable that the horse may hear the words better than the man and at the end of the story the man may laugh, but the horse will never give a horse laugh. The reason is that the horse gets only the material side of the "sacrament," namely, the sound; but the man gets the invisible or the spiritual side, namely, the meaning.

A handshake is a kind of sacrament, because there is something seen and felt, namely, the clasping of hands; but there is something mysterious and unseen, namely, the communication of friendship. A kiss is a kind of sacrament: the physical side of it is present if one kisses one's own hand, but the spiritual side of it is missing because there is no sign of affection for another. One of the reasons why a stolen kiss is often resented is that it is not sacramental; it has the carnal side without a spiritual side; that is, the willingness to exchange a mark of esteen or affection.

This book on the sacraments is written because men live in a world that has become entirely too serious. Gold is gold, nuclear warfare is nuclear warfare, dust is dust, money is money. No significance or meaning is seen in the things that make a sound to the ear, or a sight to the eye. In a world without a divine sense of humor, architecture loses decoration and people lose courtesy in their relationships with one another.

When civilation was permeated with a happier philosophy, when things were seen as signs of outward expression of the unseen, architecture was enhanced with a thousand decorations: a pelican feeding her young from her own veins symbolized the sacrifice of Christ; the gargoyle peering from behind a pillar in a cathedral reminded us that temptations are to be found even in the most holy places. Our Lord, on the occasion of His planned entrance into Jerusalem, said that if men withheld their praise of Him, "the very stones would cry out," which they did as, later, they burst into Gothic Cathedrals.

Now the stones are silent, for modern man no longer believes in another world; they have no story to tell, no meaning to convey, no truth to illustrate. When faith in the spiritual is lost, architecture has nothing to symbolize; similarly when men lose the conviction of the immortal soul, there is a decline in the respect for the human. Man without a soul is a thing; something to be used, not something to be reverenced. He becomes "functional" like a building, or a monkey wrench, or a wheel. The courtesies, the amenities, the urbanities, the gentility that one mortal ought to have for another are neglected once man is no longer seen as bearing withing himself the Divine Image. Courtesy is not a condescension of a superior to an inferior, or a patronizing interest in another's affairs; it is the homage of the heart of the sacredness of human worth. Courtesy is born of holiness, as ornamentation is born of the sense of the holy. Let us see if ornamentation returns to architecture, if courtesy also returns to human manners; for by one and the same stroke, men will have lost their dull seriousness, and will begin to live in a sacramental universe with a divine sense of humor.

Life is a vertical dimension expressed in the soaring spire, or in the leaping fountain, both of which suggest that earth, history, and nature must be left behind to seek union with the Eternal. Opposite to this is an error which substitutes the horizontal for the vertical, the prostrate form of death for the upright stature of life. It is the disease of secularity and of naturalism. It insists on the ultimacy of the seen and the temporal, and the meaninglessness of the spiritual and the invisible.

Two errors can mar our understanding of the natural world: one is to cut off entirely from Almighty God; the other is to confound it substantially with Him. In the first instance, we have the clock without the clock maker, the painting without the artist, the verse without the poet. In the second instance, we have the forger and the forged rolled into one, the melting and the fusing of the murderer and the victim, the boiling of the cook and his dinner. Atheism cuts off creation from its Creator; pantheism identifies nature with God. The true notion is that the material universe is a sign or an indication of what God is. We look at the purity of the snowflake and we see something of the goodness of God. The world is full of poetry; it is sin which turns it into prose.

The Bible is a Sacramental

Coming closer to the meaning of sacrament, the Bible is a sacramental in the sense that it has a foreground and a background. In the foreground are the actors, the cult, the temple, the wars, the sufferings, and the glories of men. In the background, however, is the all-pervading presence of God as the Chief Actor, Who subjects nations to judgment according to their obedience or disobedience to the moral law, and Who uses incidents or historical facts as types, or symbols, of something else that will happen. For example, take the brazen serpent in the desert. When the Jewish people were bitten by poisonous serpents, God commanded Moses to make a brazen serpent, and to hang it over the crotch of a tree; all who would look upon that serpent of brass would be healed of the serpent's sting. This apparently was a rather ridiculous remedy for poison and not everyone looked on it. If one could divine or guess their reason, it would probably be because they concentrated on only one side of the symbol; namely, the lifeless, shiny, brass thing hanging on a tree. But it proved to be a symbol of faith: God used that material thing as a symbol of trust or faith in Him.

The symbolism goes still further. The Old Testament is fulfilled in Christ, Who reveals the full mystery of the brazen serpent. Our Lord told Nicodemus that the brass serpent was lifted up in the desert, so that He would have to be lifted up on a Cross. The meaning now became clear; the brass serpent in the desert *looked* like the serpent that bit the people; but though it *seemed* to be the same, it was actually *without* any poison.

Our Blessed Lord now says that He is like that brazen serpent. He, too, would be lifted up on the crotch of a tree, a Cross. He would look as if He Himself was filled with the poison of sin, for His Body would bear the marks, and the stings, and the piercing of sin; and yet as the brass serpent was without poison so He would be without sin. As those who looked upon that Brass serpent in the desert in faith were healed of the bite of the serpent, so all who would look upon Him on His Cross bearing the sins and poisons of the world would also be healed of the poison of the serpent, Satan.

The word "sacrament" in Greek means "mystery," and Christ has been called by St. Paul "the mystery hidden from the ages." In Him is something divine, something human, something eternal, something temporal; something invisible, something visible. The mystery of Bethlehem was the Son of God taking upon Himself a human nature to unite human nature and divine nature in one Person. He Who, in the language of Scripture, could stop the turning about of the Arcturus, had the prophecy of His birthplace determined, however unconsciously, by a Caesar ordering an imperial census. He Who clothed the fields with grass, Himself was clothed with swaddling bands. He from Whose hands came planets and worlds had tiny arms that were not quite long enough to touch the huge heads of the cattle. He Who trod the everlasting hills was too weak to walk. The Eternal Word was dumb. The Bird that built the nest of the world was hatched therein.

The human nature of Our Blessed Lord had no power to sanctify of and by itself; that is to say, apart from its union with divinity. But because of that union, the humanity of Christ became the efficient cause of our justification and sanctification and will be until the end of the world. Herein is hidden a hint of the sacraments. The humanity of Christ was the bearer of divine life and the means of making men holy; the sacraments were also to become the effective signs of the sanctification purchased by His death. As Our Blessed Lord was the sensible sign of God, so the sacraments were to become the sensible signs of the grace which Our Lord had won for us.

If men were angles or pure spirits, there would have been no need of Christ using human natures or material things for the communication of the divine; but because man is composed of matter and spirit, body and soul, man functions best when he sees the material as the revealer of the spiritual. From the very beginning of man's life, his mother's fondling is not merely to leave an impress upon his infant body, but rather to communicate the sublimely beautiful and invisible love of the mother. It is not the material thing which a man values, but rather what is *signified* by the material thing. As Thomas a Kempis said, "regard not so much the gift of the lover as the love of the giver." We tear price tags from gifts so that there will be no material relationship existing between the love that gave the thing and the thing itself. If man had no soul or spiritual destiny, then communism would satisfy. If man were only a biological organism, then he would be content to eat and to sleep and to die like a cow.

What the Sacraments Bring to Man

The sacraments bring divine life or grace. Christ's reason for taking upon Himself a human nature was to pay for sin by death on the cross and to bring us a higher life: "I have come so that they may have life and have it more abundantly" (John 10:10). But it may be said, that man already has life. Indeed he does; he has a biological, physiological life. He once had a higher divine life which he lost. Christ came to bring that life back to man. This higher life which is divine, distinct from the human, is called grace, because it is *gratis* or a free gift of God.

Two tadpoles at the bottom of a pond were one day discussing the problem of existence. One said to the other, "I think I will stick my head out to see if there is anything else in the world." The other tadpole said, "Don't be silly, do you think there is anything else in this world besides water?" So those who live the natural life ignore the beauty of the higher life of grace.

Man may live at three different levels: the sensate, the intellectual, and the divine. These may be likened to a three-story house. The *sensate* level, or the first floor, represents those who deny any other reality except the pleasures that come from the flesh. Their house is rather poorly furnished and is capable of giving intermittent thrills which quickly dry up. The occupant of this first floor is not interested in being told of higher levels of existence; in fact, he may even deny their existence.

On the second floor, there is the *intellectual* level of existence, that of the scientist, the historian, the journalist, the humanist; the man who has brought to a peak all of the powers of human reason and human will. This is a much more comfortable kind of existence, and far more satisfying to the human spirit. Those on the second floor may think their floor is "a closed universe," regarding as superstitious those who desire a higher form of life.

But there is actually a third floor which is the floor of *grace* by which the human heart is illumined by truths which reason cannot know; by which the will is strengthened by a power quite beyond all psychological aids, and the heart is entranced with the love which never fails; which gives a peace that cannot be found on the two lower levels.

There is light outside the window, but it is up to man to open the blinds. The opening of the blinds does not constitute light; it is rather the condition of its entrance. When God made us, He gave us *ourselves*. When He gives us grace, He gives us *Himself*. When He created us, He gave Himself to us in a way which makes us one with Him.

One often sees signs painted on roadways, "Jesus Saves." Now this indeed is true, but the important question is how does He save? What relation have we in the twentieth century to Christ in the first? Do we establish contact with Him only by reading about Him? If that be all, our relationship is not much closer than that which we can have with Plato. If Christ is only a memory of someone who lived centuries ago, then it is rather difficult to see that His influence will be any different than that of Socrates or Buddha.

The answer to the question of how Christ saves is to be found in the sacraments. The divine life of Christ is communicated through His Church or His Mystical Body in exactly the same way that His divine life was communicated when He walked on earth. As He then used His human nature as the instrument of divinity, and used material things as signs and symbols of the conferring of His pardon, so He now uses other human natures and material things as the instruments for the communication of that some divine life.

In the earthly life of Our Lord, we read that there were two kinds of contact. There was the *visible* contact with humanity by which His power was communicated to the palsied man and to the blind, both of whom He touched. But there was also the invisible contact, in which Our Blessed Lord showed His power by working miracles at a distance, such as the curing of the servant of the centurion of Nazareth. The second kind of contact is an anticipation of the way that Christ, Who is now in heaven, extends and communicates His power through the sacraments.

Seven Conditions of Life

The physical or the natural life requires seven conditions, five of which refer to the person as an individual, the other two as members of society. The five conditions of leading an individual life are: (1) In order to live, one must obviously be born; (2) He must nourish himself, for he who does not eat shall not live; (3) He must grow to maturity, throwing away the things of the child, and assume the responsibilities of adult life; (4) In case he is wounded, he must have his wounds bound and healed; and (5) In case he has disease (for a disease is very different from a wound), the traces of the disease must be driven out. As a member of society two further conditions are required: (1) He must live under government and justice in human relationships, and (2) He is called to propagate the human species.

Over and above this human life, there is the divine Christ-life. The seven conditions of leading a personal Christ-life are the following: (1) We must be spiritually born to it, and that is the Sacrament of Baptism; (2) We must nourish the divine life in the soul, which is the Eucharist; (3) We must grow to spiritual maturity and assume full responsibilities as members of the spiritual army of the Church, which is Confirmation; (4) We must heal the wounds of sin, which is Penance; (5) We must drive out the traces of the diseases of sin, which is the Anointing of the Sick; (6) We must live under the spiritual government of the Church, which is Holy Orders; (7) We must prolong and propagate the Kingdom of God on earth, which is Matrimony. Every sacrament has an outward or visible sign, for example, in Baptism it is water, in the Eucharist it is bread and wine. But the sacrament also has a *form* or *formula,* or words of spiritual significance given to the *matter* when it is conferred. Three things then are absolutely required for a sacrament: (1) Its institution by Christ; (2) An outward sign; and (3) the Power of conferring the grace or divine life purchased for us by the Passion, Death, and Resurrection of Christ.

The Power and Efficacy of the Sacraments

The sacraments derive their power and efficacy from the Passion, Death, and Resurrection of Our Lord. Why was a blood sacrifice required to bring us the seven-fold sanctification? For several reasons: Life is in the blood, but so also is sin. The sins of the alcoholic, the libertine, and the pervert are often written on their faces; their excesses are recorded in every cell of their body and every drop of their blood. If, therefore, sin is to be done away with, there should be some shedding of blood, as if to symbolize the emptying of sin. It is often the death of soldiers that brings freedom to a nation; it is the giving of one's blood to another which heals him of anemia. The blood bank from which others may draw healing is hint of another blood bank from which souls may be healed of the ravages of sin.

Furthermore, blood is the best symbol of sacrifice, because blood is the life of man: when man gives up his blood, he gives up his life. Hence, St. Peter writes:

What was the ransom that freed you from the vain observances of ancestral tradition? You know well enough that it was not paid in earthly currency, silver or gold; it was paid in the precious Blood of Christ; no lamb was ever so pure, so spotless a victim.

(I Peter 1:18,19)

The blood of Christ had infinite value because He is a divine person. The life of a lamb is more precious than that of a fly, and the life of a man is more precious than the life of a beast, and the life of the God-Man is more precious than the life of any human being.

Our mind, our will and our conscience become completely sanctified through the application of the merits of Christ.

"Shall not the Blood of Christ, Who offered Himself, through the Holy Spirit, as a Victim unblemished in God's sight, purify our consciences, and set them free from lifeless observances, to serve the Living God?"

(HEB. 9:14)

The Application to the Sacraments

Calvary is like a reservoir of divine life or grace. From it, there flow seven different kinds of sanctification for man in different stages of his spiritual existence. Each of these seven channels is a sacrament by which the power of the Risen Christ is bestowed on souls by a spiritual and effective contact. This divine life pours into the soul when we receive the sacrament, unless we put an obstacle in the way, just as water will not flow out of a faucet if we put our hand in front of the faucet. But a faucet in a house has no power to quench thirst unless there is a reservoir and a pipeline. So the sacraments do not confer grace as magical signs; they communicate it only because they are in contact with the Risen Christ.

What makes the difference between the sacraments is how each is applied to us. The Christ-life affects us in a different way when we are born than when we are about to die; in a different way when we reach the age of responsibility than when we enter into marriage; in a different way when we wound ourselves than when we exercise government. The sunlight is the same whether it shines on mud to harden it or on wax to soften it. It shines on some flowers and makes them grow; it shines on a wound and heals it. So too, the blood of

Christ applied at different moments of life results in a different kind of power.

A principle of philosophy states: "Whatever is received is received according to the mode of the one receiving it." If you pour water into a blue glass, it looks blue; if you pour it into a red glass, it looks red. If you pour water into the parched earth, it is quite different than water poured onto a carpet or into oil. So too, when the blood of Christ and its merits flood in upon the soul, it depends upon the one receiving it. Does the soul come for strengthening? For nourishment? For healing? For a long journey? For induction into the spiritual army? The effects will differ as to whether a person is spiritually dead or spiritually living. If a member of the Church is spiritually dead, then it will revive him as does the Sacrament of Penance, or the Sacrament of Baptism.

† 10 †

The Authority of the Church

Christ is God and God is Truth. Therefore, His teaching, whether communicated through His physical body or through His Mystical Body, must be necessarily true, or infallible. It remains now to show that what is true of Christ as Teacher is true also of Christ as King.

When He came to earth in the form and likeness of man, He exercised the power and authority of God as King not only of men, but of all created things. He showed His power over nature, as He stilled the seas and the wind, and made the dead walk in the newness of life; He showed His power over angels, as He told timid apostles that He could summon legions of them to His assistance. He promised to exercise this power later on through another body, the nucleus of which would be the apostles under the headship of Peter, who were to be made one with one another and one with Him by the descent of His Holy Spirit. As unto that body and His Vicar, Peter, He communicated His Truth, so unto it He communicated also His power and His authority.[1] "All power is given to Me in heaven and in earth. . . . Going therefore teach ye all nations . . . to observe all things whatsoever I have commanded you; and behold I am with you all days even to the consummation of the world." "As the Father hath given Me commandment, so do I." "As the Father hath sent Me, I also send you." "He that believeth and is baptized shall be saved; but he that believeth not shall be condemned." "He that heareth you, heareth Me; and he that despiseth you, despiseth Me; and he that despiseth Me, despiseth Him that sent Me."

When this apostolic body under the headship of Peter on the day of Pentecost exercised authority, they did so in the name of Christ.[2] The ascension and glorification of Christ at the right

[1] What is indeed remarkable about our Lord communicating this power to the Apostles is the similarity between it and the conferring infallibility on Peter. All the Apostles were present on that occasion, but our Lord addressed Peter in the singular, "And I say to thee: thou art Peter . . . and I will give to *thee* the keys of the kingdom of heaven . . . and whatsoever *thou* shalt bind upon earth, it shall be bound also in heaven: and whatsoever *thou* shalt loose on earth, it shall be loosed also in heaven" (*Matt*. xvi. 18, 19). The keys were given to Peter alone; Peter alone was to be the rock; he alone was to feed the lambs and shepherd the sheep; he alone, would be preserved from errors of faith by the prayer of Christ, *but* the authority which Christ gave him as Head would be shared by the other apostles as long as they were with him and under his headship. And so it is that we find our Lord saying to the other apostles the plural of one of the injunctions to Peter alone: "Whatsoever *you* shall bind upon earth, shall be found also in heaven; and whatsoever *you* will loose upon earth, shall be loosed also in heaven: (*Matt*. xviii. 18). The same words, but they were first said to *Peter alone, apart* from the other apostles; then they were said to all the apostles, but *united to Peter*—hence the Vicar of Christ cannot be separated from the Bishops, neither can the Bishops be separated from the Vicar of Christ. They are united and dependent. Such is the meaning of the hierarchy of the Church. Peter was chosen and then the Church built upon him. The Church was not founded and then Peter taken from it. The foundation rock is first, then the edifice. It is in union with Peter that the Church derives its visible unity. The principle of unity precedes the things to be unified; the subject of a painting is chosen before the colours; the idea comes before the words to express it, and the plan before the building. The other apostles were one with Peter. The mission of all of them was the same; they were all divinely chosen, but they were not all of equal authority.

[2] The apostles accordingly acted in His name (*Acts* ii. 23, viii. 12–16; *Eph*. iv. 7–11). More particularly they exercised the triple power: legislative, judicial, and executive in His name. Legislative: "For it hath seemed good to the

hand of the Father did not mean that He relinquished His power and his authority any more than He relinquished His truth. It only meant that instead of governing through an individual human nature, He began to govern through co-operative human natures: His Mystical Body, the Church. While living in His physical body He exercised His power through the touch of a finger, the motion of His hand, the sound of His voice, all of which were acts of God.

Now that He lives in His Mystical Body, His power and authority remain the same; the only difference is that now He manifests it through human natures such as the apostles and those who have succeeded them even to our day, namely, the Bishops of the Church. They are to Christ in His glory much like His physical body was to Him during His earthly pilgrimage. In those days the power of God rang out in a voice to the storming sea: "Be calm"; in our day that same power rings out in the voice of a successor of the apostles—the power behind the voice remaining always the same. If the Kingship of Christ could be hidden in the form of a helpless babe, why can it not be equally hidden in the form of a Peter, a James, or a John? If God can communicate His power to a human nature made one with His Divine person in the Incarnation, why can He not continue to communicate it through other human natures made one with him by the unifying Spirit of Pentecost? Is God so limited by His creation that He cannot act through a corporate body as well as through a physical body? If men were pure spirits without bodies, then the Divine Son would never have taken on a human nature to have revealed only through the material, God revealed His invisible power through a visible human nature. But are we who live posterior to the Incarnation

---

Holy Ghost and to us, to lay no further burdens upon you" (*Acts* xv. 28, see *Matt.* xxviii. 18–20). Judicial: "And Jesus said to them: Amen I say to you, that you who have followed Me, in the regeneration, when the Son of Man shall sit on the seat of His Majesty, you also shall sit on twelve seats, judging the twelve tribes of Israel" (*Matt.* xix. 28). Executive: "I have told before, and foretell as present and now absent, to them that sinned before, and to all the rest, that if I come again, I will not spare" (2 *Cor.* xiii. 2). "And if he will not hear them: tell the Church. And if he will not hear the Church, let him be to thee as the heathen and publican (*Matt.* xviii. 17)

in any less need of a continued visible revelation of that power than was those who saw Him in the flesh? If God has chosen to reveal His invisible Divinity through a visible body, why should He suddenly stop that condescension? Once that human nature was glorified in heaven, why should He not continue to manifest Himself through other human natures made one by His Spirit of Truth? His Mystical Body, the Church, is therefore the very thing we should expect of a goodness of God, for it is modelled upon the plan of the Incarnation. It, too, is a union of the Divine and the human, the visible and the invisible, the spiritual and the material, in which Christ is the Eternal King and the Power of God.

If I am scandalized at the thought that Christ gives His power to the apostles and their successors, why should I not be more scandalized that the power of God once manifested itself in a human nature that could be nailed to a cross? If I am scandalized that the bishops of the Mystical Body exercise power in His name, then why should I not be scandalized that the power of God should teach the doctors of the law in the form of a child only twelve years of age? How else could this power and authority be preserved except by communicating it to a new body which would preserve it because it was filled with His Holy Spirit? A book could not preserve His authority, for the book needs interpretation, and who would interpret it? There has never been a society without a government, a family without a head, a nation without a ruler, or a body without a brain; and in each instance the authority is vested not in a code or a constitution, but in a person who safeguards, applies and judges it. Only a living body united with Christ as branches and vine can meet the demands of living men and women. And there is no more reason for doubting the authority of the bishops of that body, to whom the fulness of His power was communicated, than there is for doubting that the voice of Christ, who once spoke a crude Galilean dialect to His fishermen, was in very truth the Voice of God.

The Church is not a vague brotherhood or a vacuous "good fellowship" without external ties; it is a Divine-human society, a hierarchy, a spiritual organism with a subordination of part to part under the headship of Christ. The authority of this body is not from below, but from above. The apostles did not choose Christ, but Christ chose the apostles. The bishops who are their successors are not chosen by the people, it is the Mystical Body under Christ's Vicar that chooses them. Their authority therefore is not in a horizontal line with authority of priests and people; it is in a vertical line extending downwards from God to Christ and from Christ to the apostles and from the apostles to them. The bishops throughout the world therefore are not to be regarded as the police of a central government and therefore mere accidents in a plan, who might be displaced at the will of the Head. Rather they enter into the very substance of the Mystical Body as the nerves of the body enter into the very substance of a brain, or as children enter into the very notion of a family, as citizens into the notion of a state. Christ is in the bishops somewhat as the Father who sent Him is in Christ. The penetrating type-union (*circumincession,* in the language of theology) by which the Father is in the Son and the Son is in the Father is the exemplar of the union between Christ and His apostle-bishops. "I am in My Father and you in Me, and I in you."[3]

The authority of the bishops is not theirs; it is His who chose them and sent them. The power they exercise over their priests and people is not personal to them; they are merely the ambassadors of Christ. When the vicar teaches, Christ teaches; when the bishops govern, it is Christ the King who rules. To every Catholic the command of the bishops within his own sphere is in this sense the command of our Lord Himself. When bishops speak as shepherds of their flocks we do not see them; we see

---

[3] *John* xiv. 20—the same circumincession is to be found in a more particular way in (1) *Ubi Petrus, ibi ecclesia* and (2) the bishop in his diocese. What Peter is to the universal Church that the bishop is to his diocese. St. Cyprian tells us "Christian, you ought to know that the bishop is in His Church and the Church is in its bishop" (Ep. lxix). The Father is in His Son as His consubstantial splendour, as Christ is in His Church as His fulness and plentitude, and as the bishop is in his diocese as the fecundity of his priestly pontificate. Herein is the reason why the Church never abandons the titles to dioceses in which the faithful and clergy no longer reside—*in partibus infidelium.* The diocese may still be without priests or faithful, but it still lives in its bishops, like a father who has hopes of an heir. The torch of the diocese still burns because its episcopal chair is still occupied.

Christ who gave them power; they are not opaque, like curtains; they are transparent, like window-panes; we see the Divine Christ through them as the women of Jerusalem saw Divinity through the bleeding face and cross-torn body of a Man on the road to Calvary. When then the bishops of the Church in union with Peter give commands to the universal Church, their authority is for us in the truest sense of the word the very authority of Christ. The lifting of my hand in obedience to an act of the will is only the visible expression of the invisible resolution; so too the commands of the Church are the visible expressions of the invisible Christ. We would think it just as serious to disobey their legitimate authority in the Mystical Body as it would be for us to disobey Christ if we saw Him in His physical body along the shores of Galilee. They are the very voice of Christ ringing through His Mystical Body, the kingly branches of Him, the King Vine, the apostles of Him who is Apostolicity, the shepherds of Him who is the Shepherd of all—and whatsoever they bind on earth shall be bound also in heaven, and whatsoever they loose on earth shall be loosed also in heaven. If we deny this, then we shall have to deny Christ, who certainly meant what he said, in saying: "My power I give unto you. . . . He that heareth you, heareth Me. . . . And behold I am with you all days even to the consummation of the world." Take away the apostles and the first words are meaningless; take away the bishops who are their successors and the second words are vain. Accept both apostles and bishops and the words are meaningful. And so it happens once more that without the Church the gospels would be an enigma. It is the Church which makes the Gospels clear.

There are three characteristics of the Church's authority: It is *impersonal* in its visible expression; it is *divine* in its essence; and it is *free* in its effect. The authority of the Church is impersonal. That is, the lawfully constituted apostolic body does not possess authority in its own name, but only because it is representative of Christ Himself. The executive, judicial, and legislative functions of the episcopacy do not belong to any bishop as an individual person, however great the profundity of his learning or the sanctity of his life. The human natures in the Church are impersonal in their office as governors; they are merely the instruments of the Mystical Personality of Christ. Our Blessed Lord in the Incarnation assumed a human nature but not a human personality. There was only one Person in Christ—the Person of God. Hence every action of His human nature, every command, every law, every precept, belonged to His Divine Person as the Word of God. Now this impersonal character of His human nature He has communicated to His corporate nature, the Church—His Mystical Body. Just as the action of the pencil in writing is not to be attributed to the nature of the pencil but to the person writing, so is the action of the episcopacy in the Mystical Body of Christ not to be attributed to the human natures who govern, but to the Person whose instruments they are, Christ, the Eternal King. The apostles and their successors are merely the voice of Christ, the spokesmen of the Invisible Head, and the mouthpieces of the Word Incarnate. It is therefore a great error to say : "I do not want a Church, or a Pontiff, or a bishop to stand between Christ and me." The Supreme Court, the Congress, and the President do not stand between the authority of the United States and me. These three bodies are the Government of the United States and they derive their powers from the consent of the governed. The Church is even less of an intermediary because her authority comes not from below as in human governments, but from God. The Church does not come between Christ and me. The Church is Christ—*the total, permanent Christ of the centuries*. The human instruments of Christ the King are therefore to be judged not by themselves, but by Him who sent them in His name, just as the general is to be judged not by the tone of his voice but by his right to command. "He that heareth you, heareth Me," said our Lord. These words imply that He, Christ the King, would govern through others, and that those who accepted the commands of those whom He sent would be obeying Him. The commands are the words of human natures, but the authority is the authority of God.

When, therefore, the episcopacy under the headship of Peter binds and looses, rules and governs, we always look to the Person of Christ behind it, just as when we hear a voice on the radio we always look for its source, not in the machine which communicated it, but in the living person who sent it forth. It may happen that the human failings of one exercising authority may make it difficult to envisage Christ speaking through him, but that should not make us doubt that Christ speaks any more than static on our own radio makes us doubt that the tones of the one who speaks from the studio are clear and distinct.

Simon was a weak man, but Peter was the rock. The man is not the office, the person is not the message. Why have the later successors of Peter, after the manner of our Lord who changed Simon's name to Peter, dropped their family names to receive a Christian name like Leo, Pius, or Gregory; and why do the successors of the apostles, the bishops throughout the Church, under the same inspiration drop their family names whenever they are prayed for in the Memorial of Christ's Passion and Death, if it were not to remind themselves and us, that their authority is impersonal; that they are only the instruments and representatives, and that even in the strongest of their commands the words of our Lord ring for ever: "One is your master—Christ."?

The second characteristic note of the authority of the Church is that it is *Divine*. This follows from the fact that those who exercise authority are merely the representatives of Christ; they have no rights over the Kingship of Christ and cannot alter either His laws or the end and purpose of their existence, namely, the salvation of souls. In other words, the Church, because her authority is Divine, must be intolerant: the two ideas are inseparable. If we are shocked at hearing that the Church must be intolerant about the truths committed to her it is because we have lost all respect for the uniqueness of truth. It is too often generally assumed that tolerance is always right and intolerance always wrong. This is not really so. Tolerance and intolerance apply to two totally different things. Tolerance applies only to persons, but never to principles; intolerance applies only to principles but never to persons. We must be absolutely intolerant about the truths of mathematics, but we must be tolerant to the mathematician. We must not be broad-minded when we receive our bills and say that twenty and twenty *may* make sixty, but we must be tolerant to the grocer who makes the error. Nothing is so fearfully exclusive as truth. We must be intolerant about truth for that is God's making and not ours. We must be tolerant to persons for they are human and liable to error—perhaps their education, their training, their want of opportunity for learning, or their inherited prejudices and bigotries, received in good faith, keep them from knowing the truth. Most bigots are not to blame; they hate only because they have never been given an opportunity to know, and therefore never an opportunity to love. I dare say that most of us Catholics, if we were trained on as much false history as many of them, and if we had heard only lies about the Church since childhood, and had never been given an occasion to know the Church at first hand, would probably hate her as much as they do. They do not really hate the Church; they hate only that which they mistakenly believe to be the Church. To them, therefore, we must be tolerant, kind, and sympathetic. We must even pray for them as Christ prayed for those who nailed Him to the cross. But about the truths of the Church we must be intolerant, for they are divine.

Intolerance is essential when truths are at stake, otherwise, we would degenerate into the spineless inconsistency of jelly. The stronger the life, the stronger the skeleton; the more divine the truth, the more intolerant we must be about the error. The truths of the Church are the truths of Christ, and are therefore divine. The Church consequently has no power to change them. Human institutions may change their creeds and beliefs because they are man-made. But the truths of the Church are God-made, and hence many may not unmake them. The Church is merely the trustee of the talents, and when the Bridegroom cometh she must not only return to Him the original deposit of truth, but she must also show an interest on them in the increased harvest of those who have faith in His Word. Her jealousy of truth is merely the love of the Master who died rather than compromise the Truth received from His heavenly Father. Heaven and earth might pass away, but His Word would not pass away. Those who would not believe it would be condemned. This did not mean contempt for persons, for He loved all men. When He spoke this and when He called Herod a "fox" and the Pharisees a "brood of vipers" and "whitened sepulchres," He was not showing His hatred of these persons, but only showing His tremendous love for the truth which they so willfully rejected.[4] Neither in His historical existence nor in His Mystical existence in His Church does He force belief, for belief must be free; but once incorporated into His body no one may accept some of the truths and reject others. They are an organic whole and to deny one is to deny all, just as to cut an electric cable at any one point is to break the communication of its energy.[5] It may seem harsh to the outside world that the Church should be so intolerant of error, but that is not because the Church is narrow; it is only because she is a lover of truth. A heresy is like a poison in an organ of the human body,

[4] St. Paul reminds the Corinthians that they constitute one of the trials of the Church, by which she works out his salvation: "For there must be also heresies; that they also, who are approved, may be made manifest among you" (*Cor.* xi. 19). In his epistle to the Galatians he contrasts the works of the spirit and the works of the flesh, and among the latter he numbers "heresies" (*Gal.* v. 20). St. Peter, who was divinely authorized to be the rock against heresies, was familiar with them during his own lifetime. "But there were also false prophets among the people even as there shall be among you, lying teachers who shall bring in sects of perdition and deny the Lord who bought them: bringing upon themselves swift destruction: (*2 Peter* ii. 1). St. Paul commanded his fellow worker Titus to avoid them. "A man that is a heretic, after the first and second admonition, avoid: (*Titus* iii. 10).

[5] The Church is made up of individuals but not of individualities. Being a divine human organism whose soul is the Holy Spirit, the life of any individual member depends on his obedience or subservience to the life of the whole. No cell of the human body can live in its perfection apart from the organism, but the organism can live without the cell. The cell lives its own individual life because of its incorporation into the organic life, and the baptized members of the Church live their spiritual lives because one with the Body of Christ. Individuality as expressed in the attempt to grow by cutting oneself off from the Mystical Body is just as fatal as in the biological order. For example, if a portion of a kidney is removed from its connective tissue and placed in a test tube with a nutrient member it will grow, but grotesquely. In the body its growth was orderly and limited, but when removed from social control its growth develops into unspecialized tissues which lose their quality as a kidney. It could be a kidney only on one condition of its corporate fellowship with the rest of the body. So, too, the attempt to live in isolation from the Mystical Body by refusing to accept its corporate control or authority, results not only in unregulated development but in a degeneration of specialized function. The only way to avoid the peril of overestimating both ourselves and our ideas and our abilities as individuals is to keep them balanced by the authority which governs the regenerate society. That is why all heresies are nothing more or less than a gross exaggeration of a truth, and its over-emphasis, because isolated from other truths which counterbalance it.

endangering the life of the organism. Just as the human body must sometimes submit to the amputation of a diseased member in order to preserve the life of the body, so, too, the Church must occasionally amputate some of the erroneous members of the Mystical Body who refuse to accept Divine truth—because they endanger the health of the Body of Christ, and that amputation is called an excommunication. If we thought just as much of eternal truth as we do of human life we would think heresy just as serious as disease; and if we loved eternal truth—as we ought—more than human life, then we would think excommunication more necessary than amputation. The body is worth more than the raiment, the soul is worth more than the body. But though the heresy is condemned it does not follow that the heretic is lost. Due reparation made, the Church will always accept a heretic back into the treasury of her souls, but never the heresy into the treasury of her wisdom.

The third characteristic of the authority of the Church is its freedom. This statement may seem strange not only to those who believe that the authority of the Church is enslaving, but also to those who think liberty means freedom from all law and restraint. Liberty, it must be clearly understood, does not mean freedom from law; rather, obedience to law is the condition of all freedom. Aviators are free to fly only on condition that in the construction of their machine they respect the law of gravity; we are free to use words only on condition that we accept the standard meaning of those words and the authority of the dictionary; we are free to drive automobiles on the street only on condition that we obey the traffic laws; an artist is free to draw a triangle only on condition that he respects its intrinsic nature and draw it with three sides—if in a sweep of broadmindedness he drew a triangle with four sides he would very soon discover he was not free to draw a triangle at all. Every traveller who follows a road submits to a restriction of his freedom. The road limits his freedom, for if it were not for it, the whole forest primeval would be his road; but in submitting to the limitation of a road he finds he is more free to travel.

So it is with the laws of the Church. They are limitations imposed on us by Christ, it is true, but obedience to them is the gateway to freedom. The Church does not dam up the river of thought; she builds dams to prevent it from overflowing and ruining the countryside of sanity. She does not build great walls around rocky islands in the sea in order to prevent her children from playing; she builds them to prevent her children from falling into the sea and thus making all play impossible. If obedience to law is the condition of freedom, it follows that the more we obey the laws which make for our perfection, the more free we become; and the more we disobey those immanent laws which make for our development the more enslaved we become. In the physical order, for example, if I judge freedom to be exemption from the laws of health, the more I enslave and weaken myself. If in a stroke of false liberty I eat as much as and whatever I please, drink as much as and whatever I please, my health is destroyed and I thus become less free to enjoy my life. I become a slave to my ailments. Self-determination of this sort means self-termination. What the laws of health are to the physical order, truth is to the intellectual order. The more I submit myself to the truths of geography, the more free I am to travel; the more I bow down to the necessities of mathematics, the more free I am to know the stars and the secrets of the universe; and, on the contrary, the more I reject the truths of history, the more I become enslaved to ignorance. This is precisely what our Lord meant when He said: "The truth will make you free."

Now we are not only physical beings like animals; we are not only rational beings limited to the knowledge of our weak reason, we have been called to be the children of God, partakers of His Divine knowledge. It follows than that the more I submit myself to the laws of Christ and His Church, which is the Kingdom of God on earth, the more my perfection grows and the more my freedom increases. By submitting my reason to the higher light of faith I do not enslave my reason any more than a telescope enslaves my eye; when I bow down my will to the law of Calvary, I do not surrender my liberty any more than an acorn loses its nature when it dies to itself to be reborn in the oak; when I obey the truths of the teaching authority of the Church I no more relinquish my freedom than I relinquish my freedom of writing when I submit to the laws of grammar.

When I obey the commands of the Mystical Body of Christ, I am obeying that which makes me perfect not only in my body, because it subjects it to reason, not only in my mind, because it subjects it to the higher knowledge of faith, but perfect in my being, body and soul, because it leads me to perfect union with Him who is God. If liberty means freedom from that which restrains the joy of life, freedom from that which darkens the mind from discovering truth and binds the will to the sweetness of love, then how could I be more free than by submitting myself to the commands of Him who is Perfect Life, Perfect Truth, and Perfect Love? I become free only when I begin to possess myself, I become free only when I abdicate the slavery of death, of error, of hate—and I abdicate these only when I become a sharer in the Life of Him who has conquered them all.

Such is the liberty of the children of God; such is the freedom we, the cells of the Mystical Body, enjoy. We obey only what Christ wills through the representatives of His Body, we think only what He thinks in the ambassadors of His Body, and we love only what He loves through the shepherds of His Body. We are enslaved, if you will, but only at one point: we are slaves to the Kingship of Christ; but that one point is like the fixed point of a pendulum and from it we swing in beautiful rhythm with the freedom of Him who can do all things, and therefore can make us free from everything except the joy of having eternal bliss. Consciousness that He, the Truth, speaks through His Body alone accounts for that beautiful childlike spirit and simple obedience which we render as sheep to the Shepherds of His flock. That is why there wells up from our hearts at all their commands and burst on our lips the cry of joyful acceptance. "Speak, Lord, for Thy servant heard Thee in a physical body at Galilee; speak, Lord, for Thy servant hears Thee now in the Mystical Body which fills the world. Speak, Lord, for Thy truth makes us free from error; speak, Lord, for now we see that the root of all the liberties of the Church is the most glorious liberty of all—*the freedom to become a saint.*

† 11 †

What History the Stones of Notre Dame Cry Out

One of the most beautiful examples of how something material can be a symbol of the invisible is a cathedral, and especially one particular cathedral that is situated on an island. The
city of Paris, which is now divided by the river Seine, had its
beginnings on a tiny little island that lies in the center of that
river. Now called Ile de la Cité, its original Gallic name was
Lutetia, or the White City. Shaped like a great ship sunk in the
mud and run aground in the middle of a river, it fixed itself so
much on the minds of the original inhabitants that they
emblazoned it in the form of a ship on the old escutcheons of
Paris. The original Parisians called themselves *nautae,* or
boatmen. It was only later on that the city spread out from the
island to either bank of the Seine, but the Isle has always been
sacred. There the Druids built a stone monument to their gods;
there, after Caesar conquered Gaul, a new altar was erected to
Jupiter, an altar carrying the name of the Emperor Tiberius,
who reigned during the life of Christ. The little Isle continued
to be sacred soil, for it was there that St. Denis first preached
Christianity and began to convert the Gauls. A church was
built on the Isle and dedicated to the first martyr, St. Stephen.

This church, which ran along the Seine for 160 feet, finally had, in 558, a sister church built alongside it to honor the Mother of Our Lord; it was the original Notre Dame, and the last stone of it was laid in 558. By this time Our Lady was already the spiritual queen of the whole Eastern world under the title of Theotokos, or Mother of God.

Paris now spread out beyond its banks and by the twelfth century it was a thronging city of 50,000 people. What happened now on the Isle was to be decided by a peasant boy, Maurice de Sully, who about 1128 came to Paris to study. Paris was alive with argumentative life; around the doors of the church of Notre Dame students gathered for lectures and studies—and thus began the University of Paris, those who know philosophy will immediately recognize the name of the Bishop of Paris at that time: Peter Lombard. Maurice was shocked by the old church, when he compared it with some of the other churches he had seen. On feast days thousands were turned away; furthermore, it was wooden and was antiquated. It is very likely that he joined the throngs and went out to the new cathedral of St. Denis when it was dedicated and consecrated on June 11, 1144.

The cathedral had one of the largest libraries of the Middle Ages, at a time when a book cost as much as a house. Maurice de Sully spent much time among the books and became one of the most famous preachers in Paris. Many of his sermons were translated into English, and some of them today are in the Bodleian Library at Oxford. About 1159, his old mother came up from the Loire, to visit him; because of his importance, she was brought to his residence by some of the wealthy ladies of Paris, who dressed her up in what was then Parisian fashion. Maurice refused to recognize his mother and said: "My mother is a poor woman who has never worn anything but homespun." Only when she took off her rich garments did he embrace her.

In July, 1160, Peter Lombard died, and Maurice became the new Bishop of Paris. The day he assumed charge of his cathedral, he resolved to build a new church. Taking his crozier in his hand, he went out and traced on the ground the outline of the present cathedral of Notre Dame. He died thirty-six years later, and within those thirty-six years the cathedral of Notre Dame was practically completed.

Other races have had their high towers. Babylon's Tower was one of ambition, an affirmation of the humanism that is so often anti-God. The Hanging Gardens of Babylon and the Pyramids were reared to parade the pride, not of nations, but of kings. Roman towers were raised, to proclaim the victories of the legions of the eagle. The Greek temple was dedicated to reason and the American skyscraper to enterprise. But the men of the Middle Ages, in vast mass achievement, raised their cathedrals for the use of all men, the rich and the poor, and gave them to God who came to this earth through the free consent of a Woman who undid the evil done by the first woman.

The great outburst of building which characterized the Middle Ages was a direct manifestation of the upsurge of faith. When Our Lord was applauded as He entered Jerusalem, His enemies begged Him to cool off the enthusiasm of the people. Our Lord answered: "If these are silent, the stones will cry out." That was the birthday of Gothic cathedrals—all nature clamoring out in its praise of the Almighty. The applause in stone was so spontaneous that, from 1170 to 1270, 80 cathedrals and 500 churches were built in France alone.

The fundamental shape is the shape of a cross, like the old Carolingian Notre Dame and the Merovingian St. Stephen. The cathedral is oriented to the rising sun to symbolize the Light of Christ which pours into the Sanctuary in the morning. The length is 430 feet, the width at the nave and the aisles 124 feet, and the towers rise 223 feet; the cathedral can hold well over 12,000 standing and seated. The total area of the cathedral is 7,700,000 cubic feet.

The difference between the Romanesque and the Gothic styles of architecture is that, in the Gothic, builders were able to support a stone vault without the sacrifices of grace, light, and height which the Romanesque builders were forced to make. The builders of Gothic succeeded in making the ground bear the weight which had been sustained by the walls in Romanesque architecture. The result was that the walls of the Gothic church could be turned into glass, like those of our modern commercial buildings. Modern architecture and the medieval are one in this respect: the walls serve the purpose of providing shelter, not structural support. This shift of responsibility from walls to piers, which makes for lightness and grace, was the great and lasting achievement of Gothic architecture.

An interesting story is preserved about a human drama that took place during the building of the cathedral. There was a gargoyle maker who made some of the ugliest little demons ever to peer out from behind the pillars of a cathedral. The stonecutter was given to alternating between passion and sullenness as he worked out his character on the gargoyles that he carved. He tried to force himself on the wife of the designer of the Madonna window; a beautiful woman who was also the model for the Madonna window. The gargoyle maker made uncouth advances; but she didn't tell her husband about them. Finally the husband heard about it through gossips, and he sought to kill the gargoyle maker.

The designer of the window turned his wrath on his innocent wife. The gargoyle maker disappeared, and those who worked with the designer were unable to control his anger. One night, seized by a fit of rage, he took a hammer and smashed some of the principal panels of the almost finished Madonna window.

The gargoyle maker returned, and the designer threw the sculptor of the gargoyles into the Seine. The legend is that Our Lady appeared and waved toward the drowning man. Repentant, the stained-glass maker leaped into the river and bore his enemy to the shore. So the breach between the husband and wife was healed, and the new Madonna window bloomed with its rich crimson, yellows, greens, and blues, more beautiful than the window that had been shattered.

Now for some vignettes of history which took place around or inside the walls of Notre Dame. It is generally true, in our modern civilization, that the government of a people is always just a bit below the spiritual level of the best of its citizens. But in those days the highest level was found, not only among scholars like Aquinas, Bonaventure, Dante, but in a King Louis IX. One Maundy Thursday, his mother, Queen Blanche, brought her twelve-year-old son into the cathedral to see the Bishop of Paris washing the beggars' feet; she also arranged that the future King would have a towel to clean and wash at least one beggar.

As a grown man, the King would always arouse himself at midnight and recite matins at the altar before attending an early Mass; whenever he passed a church, he would dismount from his horse; in church, he never knelt at a bench to support himself.

He invited beggars to his royal table; as many as two hundred at a time would come to his dining room. He selected always the most ragged, and he would wash and kiss their feet, and carve their meat and their bread. He volunteered for bedpan duty at hospitals, and he also buried the dead. One day an old woman mocked him and said he was not fit to be a king. He said, "You surely speak the truth—I am unworthy to be a king, but if it had pleased Our Lord, He would have put someone in my place who knew better how to govern."

But not all the citizens of Paris were saints. It was around this cathedral and before the Madonna that Francois Villon loafed, made love, pilfered, and wrote verses; there, too, his mother had gone to pray for her son, the first of the modern poets, and the last great poet of the Middle Ages. He had killed a man in fighting for a girl. He was a thief, who was jailed regularly, and almost hanged; and finally he was exiled from Paris. But his old mother still made her way to Notre Dame, fell on her knees before the figure of Mary, and repeated a prayer which her son had composed: "Lady of Heaven, Regent of earth, Empress of valleys infernal, receive me your humble Christian. To your Son, say that I am His, that by Him my sins may be ended; pardon me as Mary the Egyptian, as He did for the clerk Théophile, who through You was forgiven and absolved."

Great processions passed through these doors. In 1560 Mary, Queen of Scotland, was crowned Queen Consort of France in Notre Dame. In 1687, Bishop Bossuet, the greatest orator of his time, preached the funeral oration over the brilliant Condé. In 1779, Louis XVI and his Queen, Marie Antoinette, had the square in front of the cathedral strewn with branches and flowers for a great mass marriage. One hundred poor girls, each of whom had been given a dowry, came in a body through St. Anne's door, while through the Virgin's door came 100 young grooms carrying orange blossoms. The seal of their marriage contract was stamped with the fleur-de-lis encrusted on the hilt of the sword of the King.

In 1793, revolutionists put ladders against the church and nooses were attached to the necks of the statues of twenty-eight kings, the crowd pulled them down one by one, roaring as each statue fell. With another cry, the people rushed to decapitate each crowned image, cut off hands and feet, and throw the broken torso into the Seine. The Communes of the Middle Ages built churches; the Communes of the eighteenth and nineteenth centuries and the Communists of the twentieth century have destroyed them.

On November 10, 1793, after all the statutes had been removed from the portals by revolutionists, with the exception of a few which had astronomical significance, the cathedral was taken from the patronage of Our Lady and dedicated to the goddess of Reason. A stage, transported from the opera, was set up in front of the altar. Its centerpiece was a mountain, at the peak of which was perched a statute of philosophy. Out of the Sanctuary there strutted a young actress, Mlle. Aubry, clad in a long white robe and blue mantle, armed with a spear of knowledge; tending her was a *corps de ballet* robed in white; incense was burning on the altar. The multitude in the name all sang out: "Thou, holy liberty, come dwell in the Temple, be the goddess of the French." This blasphemy aroused such enthusiasm that almost immediately 3,345 other churches were transformed into Temples of Reason. During the drunken *feast of reason* the lovely fourteenth-century Madonna next to the chancel was salvaged from the refuse pile onto which it had been thrown by the mob. The man who rescued it was Le Notre, who hid many works of art at the time to prevent them from being hacked to pieces. The Lady was later restored to her niche.

In the Revolutionary calendar, December 2, 1804, was called *Frimaire* II of the year 13. *Frimaire* means the month of shivering, and so it was, for there was snow everywhere, on the roofs of the palaces, on the gargoyles of Notre Dame, on the streets and on the porches. On that day, a state carriage drew up, and Pius VII, clad in white silk and with a white skullcap, walked down the middle aisle of the cathedral to be received by the Archbishop of Paris. Two hours later, the cannon began booming outside, announcing the arrival of Napoleon. The great cathedral bell crashed out its welcome. The Napoleonic procession of 25 carriages and 152 horses drew close to the cathedral for the coronation of Napoleon.

The consecration of kings is always a solemn ceremony. The words always used were: *Coronet vos Deus,* the idea being, as Our Lord told Pilate: "You would not have power did it not come to thee from above." But Napoleon insisted that no one had given him power; it had descended from no one; it was merely recognized by others. Hence he wanted the words to be: *Accipe coronam,* "Receive this crown." But Pius VII stood inflexibly by the principle that all power, all rights and liberties come to us from God. For this reason, Napoleon, who would recognize no power but his own, not even God's, snatched the crown from the hands of Pius VII and put it on his own head.

It was also through the forest of pillars that the voice of the greatest preacher of the nineteenth century resounded—the incomparable Lacordaire. He met with much opposition, the King himself petitioning the Archbishop that he be denied the pulpit, but the Archbishop refused to heed the appeals of the King. Often applause greeted him in church, for which he would reprimand the listeners, saying: "The word of God should be greeted by the silence of love and the immobility of respect."

In Paris today one can see what remains of the Carmes, which was destroyed by the French revolutionists and which was the scene of many martyrdoms. Lacordaire had a cell at the end of the corridor. A small window had been made from which he could look down while working and see the Tabernacle; and from the Eucharist he received the inspirations for his sermons. There is still to be seen in the basement of the Carmes a large cross on the arms of which rests a crown of thorns. In preparation for his Good Friday sermon at Notre Dame, Lacordaire would tie himself to that cross and place on his head a crown of thorns, in order that he might better prepare his soul to speak worthily of the Crucified Savior. It was before the Crucifix and the Tabernacle, rather than at his desk, that his most moving discourses were prepared.

On Christmas night, 1866, Paul Claudel, the agnostic, entered into that same cathedral, as he put it, "to draw from the Catholic ceremonial an inspiration for some decadent exercise in prose." In an instant of time, his whole life altered. All at once he felt the heart-rending experience of being a child of God. He said that the edifice of all his opinions and knowledge still continued to exist, but that he had stepped out of it. It was as if his skin had been peeled off and he were placed in a new body. There came to his mind the words of Arthur Rimbaud, "The spiritual battle is as brutal as any battle among men, O dark night! My face reeks with blood."

The Cathedral is a pattern of life, just as is the Pyramid. The Pyramid is the symbol of the totalitarian, or closed, society, where one person is like another, regardless of function, and where each is placed on another; one person holds down the other, and all are held down by a single dominating stone called the Dictator. Underneath the whole structure is a tomb, for its purpose is to house the dead in Stygian blackness; man has no other destiny than that of an ant in the anthill of the State.

The Cathedral symbolized another principle, by which persons are united according to function, with charity or love as the cement; a society in which feet are on the earth and the head is in the heavens and where light and air stream through in the beautiful harmony of freedom in fellowship.

This particular cathedral is dedicated to a Woman—so that women might have an ideal and men might have respect. She is set up, not because she is a goddess, for she is not; not because she is in any sense Divine, for she is not; but simply because it was through her portals that God came to earth. Whenever she is attacked, her Son is attacked. The Church begins with the defense of the human—and that is what she is; to adore her as we adore God would be blasphemy. But she is the outer defense, the rampart of Christian civilization. If the outer walls are taken, then the inner defenses might crumble. If she is ignored, her Son will be ignored; if the Son is denied, she will be denied—that is the logic of the relationship of Mother and Son. One cannot go to a statue of a mother holding a babe and hack away the babe, without in some way hacking the mother. She is merely the gate, she is not heaven itself; she is the moon—but she gets her light and heat, as the moon does, from a reflection: from the Sun Light Who is the Son.

† 12 †

The Three Great Confessions of History

One of our nation's major problems is mental health. But this does not mean that there is as much abnormality as is generally believed. Too often an inner conflict is identified with the abnormal. This assumption is quite unwarranted. There are some conflicts that are normal, such as the tension we feel between the aspirations of the spirit and the carnal urges of the body; then, too, there is a conflict between what we are and what we ought to be. Tension is normal in our present human condition; it is the denial of the true causes of tension which begets so many abnormal and subhuman states.

The tensions which are normal to human nature, such as having our heads in the heavens and our feet on earth, and the sense of guilt which flows from breaking a relationship with the moral order, have not always been solved in the right way. It may be helpful to discuss three lives which were disturbed by sex problems and see how they resolved the normal and the abnormal conflicts. The three types are St. Augustine, Héloïse, and Jean Jacques Rousseau.

Each person mentioned suffered from a conflict due to breaking the moral law; but no two solved the problem of guilt in the same way. The first chose the right solution, the third chose the most completely wrong one and unfortunately the one that is the most popular today.

If there ever was a man who could be said to have adored sex, it was Augustine. He said that he never could distinguish between "serene affection and black lasciviousness." His youth he described as "the hellish voluptuousness of adolescence." An unfaithful father did not give him a good example, although a saintly mother, Monica, did. In the face of the conflict between flesh and spirit, Augustine surrendered completely to the flesh. In the year 371 he took unto himself as a common-law wife an unnamed woman who bore him a son, called Adeodatus, which means "given by God." His father died the very year he took his common-law wife; he was then a famous student in the great University of Carthage, where he combined abandonment to vice with such intellectual brilliance that he was the leader of his class.

Most people justify the way they live; that is to say, instead of fitting their lives to a philosophy, they invent a philosophy to fit their lives. Inasmuch as Augustine was not true to the woman with whom he was living, and inasmuch as he had to justify his vice, he accepted the philosophy of the Manicheans, which propounded a dual principle of good and evil. The conflict between flesh and spirit in him was resolved by Manichaeanism, because it enabled him to pursue a voluptuous life without ever being held accountable for it. He could say that the evil principle within him was so strong and deep and intense that the good principle could not operate.

All the while his mother wept night and day for the mental and moral errors of her son. She went to the Bishop, who told her: "It is not possible that a son of so many tears should perish." The mother prayed that her son would never go to Italy because she feared that there would be more evil companionship there than in Northern Africa. Her prayers seemed to go unanswered, but, at the same time, they were answered in a mysterious way. In the year 384, Augustine told his mother to go to visit the church of St. Cyprian the Martyr while he went to visit friends. He slipped away from Africa that night and went to Rome. His reputation as an orator and rhetorician preceded him, and he was recognized as one of the most learned men of his time. In the year 384, when he arrived in Rome, the prefect of Rome was a certain Symmachus who was anxious to restore paganism and the Altar of Victory, which had been removed during the growth of Christianity. Symmachus felt the best advocate he could have in the imperial court, which was then Milan, would be Augustine; nobody could plead better than Augustine for the restoration of paganism.

Three influences now converged to affect his spiritual and moral life. The first was a lost work of Cicero called *Hortensius,* a dialogue on philosophy, written against those who disparaged philosophy. Augustine said that this work altered his state of mind because it revealed to him the great and hidden beauties of a life of contemplation.

The second influence was that of St. Ambrose, the Bishop of Milan. When Augustine went there, he heard of the scholarship and the oratorical powers of the prelate. Many days he would sit under the pulpit in veneration of Ambrose, but veneration always implies a distance. He later on spent many hours in his company, discussing philosophy, and he took manuscripts from his library to read. Out of the conversations with Ambrose there came two salutary resolutions on the part of Augustine. One of them to give up Manichaeanism. Monica, who had prayed that her son would never go to Italy, now came to Milan with another son, Navigius, to discover in a short time that their prayers had been answered in another way. In his family group now there were Monica, his brother Navigius, the nameless woman who was his wife, Adeodatus, who was not thirteen, and his faithful friends Alypius and Nebridius.

All the while, the chains of habit were strong in Augustine, and his carnal nature was resisting his spiritual birth. As he put it: "It is perversion of the will that creates libido; libido creates habit, and then resistance to habit creates necessity." In July, Augustine received a visit from a court dignitary whose name was Pontitianus, and who, like himself, was an African. Pontitianus told Augustine the story of St. Anthony of the Desert. This heroic anchorite had spent more than seventy years in the desert. After hearing the story, Augustine said: "Manes is an impostor. The Almighty calls me. Christ is the only way and

Paul is my guide." If Anthony had conquered the libido and sex, why could not he, Augustine asked himself. Augustine, eager to be alone, went into the garden. There he underwent a conflict between the old ego and the new one that was being born. Casting himself at the foot of a spreading fig tree, he cried hot and bitter tears which overflowed and bathed his spirit.

But the chains of earthly passions held him back, and he cried: "When shall I achieve salvation, when cast off my fetters? Tomorrow perhaps, or the day after? Why not this very hour?" And suddenly he became aware of the voice of a child, a boy or girl, he knew not, speaking in a neighboring house. "Take up and read," said the sweet voice.

He hurried back into the room. He found a copy of the Epistles of St. Paul, which Pontitianus had been fingering. Seizing it, and opening it at random, his eyes fell upon the words of St. Paul to the Romans: "Not in rioting and drunkenness, not in chambering and wantonnness, not in strife and envying; but put ye on the Lord Jesus Christ and make not provision for the flesh." In that one moment, the carnal passions which had for sixteen years appeared invincible, were annihilated.

On Holy Thursday, which fell on April 22 that year, he recited the Credo aloud in the presence of an assembled congregation. He fasted until Holy Saturday and in the evening he went to the Basilica, where Ambrose pronounced the last exorcisms over him, made the sign of the Cross upon his forehead and breast, and poured the baptismal waters.

Then in accordance with the custom used only in the church of Milan, Ambrose got on his knees and washed the feet of Augustine. The two saints were united for perhaps the last time on earth. The elder humbled himself before the younger, the more famous before the more obscure. Adeodatus, "the carnal son of his sinning," received Baptism at the same time; the nameless woman returned to Carthage and spent her remaining days in penance.

One of the effects of his conversion was a return to joviality, and a deep sense of inner peace. There was also a great increase of literary productiveness. Between the years 380 and

386, he had not written a single page. At the age of thirty-two, he had written only one book. Now, in a short space of time, he composed four brief books in succession.

In 397, or twelve years after his conversion, Augustine wrote his *Confessions,* the greatest spiritual autobiography ever written. It is the work of a teacher who explains, a philosopher who thinks, a theologian who instructs, a poet who achieves chaste beauty in the writing, and a mystic who pours out thanks for having found himself in peace. None of the Freuds or Jungs or Adlers of our generation has ever pierced the conscious and the unconscious mind with a rapier as keen as Augustine's. No man can say he has ever understood himself if he has not read the *Confessions of Augustine.*

In the first centuries after Christ the common subject of conversation was theology; in the Middle Ages, it was philosophy; today it is politics. We switch now to a time 700 years after Augustine, one of the most intellectual periods in the world's history. The place where the drama began was the old cathedral of Notre Dame in Paris, which was about to give way to the new. This famous church was not only a cathedral but a university. Men worked and preached, baptized and taught in the cloister of Notre Dame. To it came Peter Abélard, aged nineteen, fresh from his father's home in Nantes. Abélard plunged into the great intellectual battles of his time, and he had plenty of competition from Chartres, Rheims, Soissons, Fulda, Cologne, and Bologna. But he always stood out from his rivals in bold relief as though there were a spotlight on him. He had an excellent mind, a winning address, graceful gestures, handsomeness of features, and a vibrant resonance in his voice. He was considered a boy wonder; he was smart, and he had reason to know it, as thousands thronged to hear his lectures.

When he was twenty-two years of age, he was very flattered to see the great scholar and rector of the cathedral of Notre Dame who was also builder of the present cathedral. Canon Fulbert, in the audience. He was a man of prodigious learning and great charity. With the Canon sat his pretty niece, two years of age. Sixteen years later Héloïse had been taught Hebrew, Latin, Greek, scripture, theology, and philosophy by her uncle, the Canon. He engaged Abélard to continue the instruction of the pretty, vivacious, witty, and brilliant girl. Abelard was then thirty-eight. He began talking to the girl about the subtleties of scholastic philosophy, then about the weather, and finally about the beauty of the moon. It was not long afterward that he began to love Héloïse not wisely but too well; to cover the shame of her unmarried motherhood, he sent her to Brittany, where later on a child was born called Astrobal. Canon Fulbert was violently angry with Abélard and did him a grievous physical injury.

An exchange of correspondence went on after that between Héloïse and Abélard. In those days it was the men who kept the letters, and the many letters of Héloïse constitute her confessions, which have the same starting point as those of Augustine, namely the conflict of flesh and spirit. Neither Abélard nor Héloïse ever attempted to justify their mistakes, as Augustine did in his earlier days when he escaped into Manichaeanism. They both admitted that the moral law was right, and they both admitted that they had broken it. Abélard too wrote his confessions in what he called *The History of Calamities*.

Héloïse at first contended that, since Abélard had chosen the profession of scholarship, marriage was not advisable for him. Her arguments were drawn from history. One was that Cicero refused to take a wife after he divorced Terentia, because "he could not devote himself to wife and philosophy at the same time." Héloïse also pointed out that there was very little accord between philosophy and cradles, between books and playthings, between the pen that writes and the playpen. "Who, engaged in a religious or philosophical meditation, could endure a baby's crying and the nurse's ditties stilling it, and all the noise of servants? Could you put up with the dirty ways of children? The rich can say, with their palaces and apartments of all kinds, that their wealth does not feel the expense or the daily care and annoyance, but I say, the state of the rich is not that of philosophers. . . . Remember Socrates was tied to a wife, and what happened to him should be a lesson that philosophers afterward should be more cautious." She then quoted Jerome, who recounted how one day, Socrates, after enduring a story of Xanthippe's shouts from the floor above, was finally doused by his wife with a barrel of water, which prompted him to say: "I knew such thunder would bring rain." Héloïse ended up by saying: "One thing is left: in the ruin of us both, the grief which follows shall be less than the love which went before." The child was born, but later on died. Héloïse entered a convent after that, not for God's sake but for Abélard's. She gave no indication that she ever became really and spontaneously devoted to her calling. When Abélard got her to cease making accusations of cruelty against God and of egotism against Abélard himself, she agreed to be silent about those things in order to speak of other things. As she put it: "One nail drives out another and so new thoughts will drive out the old."

Abélard lost his brilliance. He had defeated many giants in debate, but now up from Clairvaux came the great Bernard, who defeated him ignominiously. He became a broken man, and he went to the abbey of Cluny, not very far from where Heloïse was living in her convent.

In 1871, the French, who have always loved the romance of Héloïse and Abélard, brought the bodies of both to Paris, and buried them in the cemetery of Père Lachaise. The heart of Héloïse may have been torn between Abélard, and God, but, in death at least, she could be reconciled with both. The conflict that was not solved clearly in life by either of them was, as all such conflicts are, resolved in death, when the spirit has survived the flesh.

Jean Jacques Rousseau was born in Geneva on June 28, 1712, and he died on July 2, 1778. His father was a watchmaker. His mother died shortly after his birth. His father used to keep him up late at night, by reading sensuous novels to him. Later on, he took refuge in the home of Mme. de Warens, who also led him along the paths of sensuality. For a brief time, he thought of religion, but then he abandoned both faith and reason; as he put it: "Even at an early age, I had acquired by this dangerous method of reading, a unique understanding of passions for my own age. I never understood anything, I just felt." In 1736, he admitted that he was a neurotic. "My passions made me live and my passions killed me. The need of loving devoured me. A bombardment went on inside me which for thirty years never left me. The total loss of sleep convinced me that there was little time to live." He lived for forty years afterward. He entered into a common-law marriage with Teresa Le Vasseur, saying he would never legally marry her, but finally he did, in the year 1768. She bore him five children, each of whom was given to charity the day after birth and abandoned by the father and mother. It should be pointed out, in passing, that Rousseau once wrote a long treatise on how to educate children.

In his celebrated work, *The Confessions,* he wrote in Book III: "Two things almost disparàte unite in me in a way which I cannot understand: a very ardent temperament, impetuous passions and ideas slow to be born and embarrassed which ever present themselves spontaneously. One would say that my heart and my mind did not belong to the same individual. I feel everything, I see nothing."

What Rousseau did was to give to the world a new concept of nature. The word "nature" as applied to humanity can be understood in at least two senses: a metaphysical sense and an historical sense. Metaphysically, it means the highest ideal and potential of humanity. In the historical sense, it means the primitive or original, that which exists before development. Rousseau takes the latter meaning. For him man is naturally good, it is civilization that makes him wicked. This idea came to him in the summer of 1749, when he was reading the *Mercure de France* while walking to Vincennes to see his imprisoned friend Diderot. He had read that the Academy of Dijon was offering a prize for the subject "Has the progress of science and arts done more to corrupt morals or improve them?" Rousseau, thinking about it, began to weep, so copiously that his waistcoat was soon wet with tears. He was overwhelmed, he said, with the greatness of his conclusion: "Man is naturally good, it is civilization that has made him wicked." Reason, according to Rousseau, is like a flickering candle, too weak to illumine the dark surge of passions; reason takes care not to interfere with man's emotions, except to use them to make vice more attractive.

The very titles he gave his books indicate an interest in the confessions of St. Augustine and of Héloïse: one was called

Confessions, another The *New Héloïse*. "The man who medi-
tates is a corrupted animal . . . reason, far from enlightening
us—blurs us. . . . Do not think. . . . Feel. . . . Provided that
you feel that I am right, I do not need to prove it to you."
Rousseau claimed that the only evil he ever did in his life was
by thinking. "I give myself up to the impression of the moment
without resistance, for I am perfectly satisfied that my heart
only loves what is good." There is no conflict within the primitive man, because man is naturally good; what might be called
evil is due therefore to "civilization."

If a man does not suit his life to an idea, he will find an idea
and suit it to his life. If we do not live as we think, we soon
begin to think as we live. So Jean Jacques, who glorified emotion, now formed a philosophy to suit his sensuality—the philosophy of Romanticism, or the glorification of the sentimental
ego.

Since there is no objective order, since man is his own best
judge, Jean Jacques now declared himself to be a saint. He set
himself to do bravely everything that seemed good to him:
"Holiness consists in loving [myself] above all things. I love
myself too much to hate anybody. I want to show my fellows a
man in all the truth of Nature; and that man will be myself. I
am made like none of those whom I have seen. . . . At the
Judgment when a countless multitude of fellow creatures
gather . . . see if any one will dare say: I was better than that
man! . . . I am convinced that of all men I have known in my
life none was better than I." He also said he would commit
suicide if he met a man better than himself. "I think that never
did any individual of our species have naturally less vanity than
I. . . . If I had been invisible like God, I should have been
beneficent and good as He is."

Jean Jacques was always innocent; no quilt, no sin, no failing; no want of natural goodness. It was the hallowing of the
denial of grace.

Rousseau was the first of the psychiatric philosophers of
modern times, not only because he denied the conflict of matter
and spirit, but also because he denied the reality of guilt. Reason was now outlawed; the person is being normal when he allows his instincts free expression. He did not say in so many

words that the "id" should master the "super-ego," because those words were not in current use; but in proclaiming the primacy of the sentimental ego, which is the basis of Romanticism, he initiated the antirational approach to mental and moral problems. There was no longer an inner conflict because of the dual nature of man; conflict was due to civilization. In the primitive state man was normal, right, and good; it was civilization that had made him wicked. The "civilization complex" is one with the "father complex" and the "mother complex" inasmuch as all three relieve the person of any responsibility.

These three Confessions reveal right and wrong solutions of the conflict of body and spirit. They can be likened to three persons seated at a piano, each with the same piece of music before him. All three strike a wrong note at the beginning, as did Augustine, Héloïse, and Rousseau, when they first deviated from the objective norm of morality. The first player, after striking a false note, looks at the music and conforms to its requirements. This is Augustine in his compliance with the moral law of God. The second, after a bad beginning, hits the right note, not because the music demands it, but out of love for the teacher. This is Héloïse, who adjusted herself to the moral law, not on account of God precisely, but because Abélard asked her to do it. The third, after hitting the wrong note, tears up the music and says: "From this time on, any note I feel like hitting is the right note."

Looking back over the three reactions to conflict, one is struck by the great difference between the mental wounds of the past and those of modern times. The sins of former days were clear wounds; wounds on white flesh; they divided neatly like the rod of Moses parting the waters of the Red Sea; the blood was healthy, and cut clean. This is because when men did wrong they admitted it, as did Augustine, Abélard, and Héloïse. But today the wounds are hidden; there is pus on the inside; something attacks the cells; there is ruin inside like a cancer, and only after it has undermined everything within does it appear on the surface. The causes of mental disease: guilt and sin, the moral order, and God, are all denied; hence all that can be treated are the superficial symptoms, not the disease itself. Some psychiatrists may deny the reality of guilt,

† 13 †

The Philosophy of Mediaeval Art

There is no such thing as understanding art in any period apart from the philosophy of that period. Philosophy inspires art, and art reflects philosophy. We can never tell what the art of an age is unless we know what is the thought of the age. If the thought is lofty and spiritual, art will be lofty and spiritual; if the thought is base and material, art will be base and material. If the thought is of the heavens heavenly, art will be of the heavens heavenly; if the thought is of the earth earthly, art will be of the earth earthly. In that period of Grecian history, for example, when Plato and Socrates and Aristotle were giving eternal truths to men, the clear lines of the Parthenon and the airy Ionic of the Erechtheion served as so many petrified incarnations of their thought. Closer to our own times, when Rousseau set loose his exaltation of the ego and the romanticism of sense-passion, artists were found drinking at his fountain the shallow drafts of hatred for academic tradition, a license of inspiration, and a glorification of fleshy sensibilities. And now in our own day, what is the philosophical inspiration of Futurism and its wild love of novelty and "absolute commencement," motion for motion's sake, but the thought of

Henri Bergson? What is the philosophical inspiration of Cubism, with its unrelated blocks, but the philosophy of Pluralism, which maintains that the multiple does not imply the unit? What is the whole inspiration of modern art but a Subjectivism introduced by Kant and his school, the heritage of which is a belief that no work of art itself is beautiful, but that it is our psychic or mental states that are beautiful, either because we project these states to the object, which is the *Einfühlung* theory, or because they harmonize with the tastes and commandments of society, which is the sociological theory, or because they produce interesting reactions, which is the Pragmatic theory?

If Modern philosophy explains modern art, mediaeval philosophy explains mediaeval art. If we are to understand why they painted and why they sculptured and why they built a certain way, we must ask ourselves how they thought, for art in the lyrical expression of philosophy. Their civilization was much different from our own; in the thirteenth century Christendom knew but one Church. There was just one Faith, one Lord, one Baptism, one Church. Since it was one in its rule of faith, it is easy to extract those basic principles of mediaeval life which served as the inspiration of their art. These principles are threefold: (1) Impersonalism, (2) Dogmatism, (3) Sacramentalism. Their thought was impersonal, and because it was impersonal, it was capable of being dogmatic, and all its dogmatism is summed up in its Sacramentalism. We shall expose these principles in contrast with modern principles, and then show how they worked themselves out in the art of that period.

Individualism is the characteristic of modern thought; impersonalism is the characteristic of medieval thought. The egocentrism of modern thought has its roots in Descartes, who in his "Discourse on Method" expressed contempt for all history and insisted that all philosophy should be made a *tabula rasa* to be written on anew. Writing to Gassendi, he said: "You forget that you speak to a man who does not wish to know if any one ever existed before him; I, I, I, that is enough." Kant, the *privat-dozent* of Konigsberg, did not suffer this individualism to die. His thought, he said, would be like a Copernican revolution in the world. This egocentrism was carried to its limits in the philosophy of Pragmatism, which makes the individual the measure of truth. What is useful is true, according to Pragmatism. If God is useful for your life, He exists for you; if He is not useful for my life, He does not exist for me. The individual is self-important. Pragmatism was a war against Truth. Truth is not transcendental, it declared; it is ambulatory. It is personal and individual.

On the contrary, for the Scholastic or the mediaevalist, truth is eternal and common. It is like a great edifice gradually built up from the accumulations of centuries. Like a great patrimony it passes from one generation to another and at no time is it considered the *personal property of him who finds it*. St. Thomas Aquinas, the master mind of this period and perhaps the master of all times, insists on this impersonal constitution of truth. Referring to that great Greek thinker, Aristotle, whom he has dignified with the title "The Philosopher," he writes: "That which a single mind can bring, through his work and genius, to the promotion of truth is little in comparison with the total of knowledge. However, from all these elements, selected and coordinated and brought together, there arises a marvelous thing, as is shown by the various departments of learning, which by the work and sagacity of many minds have come to a wonderful augmentation."

Because truth was impersonal there was a great reverence for tradition in the Middle Ages. Tradition is not, as some believe, a heritage of the Dark Ages, something that cabins and confines thought; rather, it is a memory. A sense and an intellectual memory are indispensable conditions of all right thinking. We are under the necessity of going back to the storehouse of our mind for past impressions and thoughts in order to build up the present thought. What is true of the individual is true of society. Tradition is the memory of society and without that tradition society cannot think. "It is owing to tradition," says Pascal, "that the whole procession of men in the course of so many centuries may be considered as a single mind who always subsists and who learns continually."

Because truth is impersonal and the common patrimony of mankind, the great thinkers of that time rarely referred to another thinker by his own name. Run through the "Summa" of Aquinas or the works of any of the other great thinkers such as Richard of St. Victor, Bonaventure, and Scotus, and observe the frequency of such expressions as: *"Aliquis dicit," "Unus dicit"* ("Some one says"; "They say"). St. Thomas, for example, in refuting the Anselmian *a priori* argument for the existence of God in the "Summa" does not mention Anselm's name, and although he and Bonaventure taught around the corner from each other there is no mention of the other in the writings of either. Neither does the Angelic Doctor mention even once the name of the teacher, Albertus Magnus, probably because he was enjoined by the humility of his master to keep it silent.

If thought is impersonal it will necessarily be dogmatic, that is, express itself in certain universal and general concepts. Here again there is a wide difference between the modern notion of dogma and the medieval notion and the tradition that continues it. The modern notion is that truths change with the times; that just as we discard the old phaeton of our grandfathers for the limousine of the twentieth century, so too we change grandfather's notions of morality and religion for the modern notions. Scientific progress is said to have shown the futility of old dogmas, and the microscope is said to have revealed the inanities of theology.

For the mediaevalist, on the contrary, dogmas are no more subject to change than the multiplication table. Two and two make four for the thirteenth century as well as for the twentieth, and a dogma like that of the Incarnation is as true for the twentieth as it is for the thirteenth century. Dogmas are above space and time because they are not sentimental appreciations of a sentimentalist, but intellectual truths of an intellect. Neither is theology a mere science of comparative religions. St. Thomas teaches that theology is the queen of sciences, that "it surpasses all sciences in its principles, its object, its certitude, and its end." In theology everything possesses its own objective value; it is true in itself, apart from our appreciation of it. Its dogmas are not barriers to thought. They are no more confining for a mind than plan, contour, and choice of colors are confining for an artist. No great artist ever complained about the exigencies of dogma. A dogma is for the artist what the multiplication table is for the mathematician, or the logarithms are for the calculist, or the law of gravitation is for the physicist. They are not dams that wall up the river of thought; they are breakwaters that prevent it from overflowing the country-side of sanity.

Modern thinkers are quite generally prepared to look upon this world as a lasting city and as an end rather than as a means to an end. They quote Swinburne approvingly: "Glory to man in the highest, for man is the master of all." Religion then, instead of becoming the sum of man's duties toward God, becomes the sum of God's duties toward man. A typical expression of its nature is the following, "To put the question bluntly, religion must be separated from the other-worldly pull of the traditional theologies and be sanely grounded in the outlook of modern knowledge." Earth must resume its rights, for the earth is the paradise and the end of man.

But in the perennial thought of the Scholastics, religion meant an ordination to God as our First Cause and Last end. Religion is no more intelligible without God than physics is intelligible without matter. The world, too, instead of being an end is a means to an end. In other words, the world is a great sacrament. There are seven sacraments in the supernatural order, which elevate and perfect man in the higher divine life, and in the natural order, everything can be a sacrament. A sacrament is a material thing used as a channel of spiritual sanctification, and since everything is destined to lead us to God, everything is a sacrament. The process by which matter is to be a sacramentalized is after the fashion of a pyramid, at the base of which is the material order and at the peak of which is man. There is progress and continuity in the universe. Plants consume minerals, animals consume plants, and minerals, and man consumes all three. Thus, physically, there is within man the whole material universe.

But there is yet another way than the physical one by which he possesses all orders below him, and that is by knowledge. Because man has a spiritual soul he can know all things and thus contain all things within himself in a spiritual way. Hence man is destined to become not only a microcosm, as Aristotle

tells us, but a living voice for all creation. He is to be the
spokesman of the minerals, the plants, and the animals, for the
very reason that he sums up all these orders. He is to lead them
all back to God. The mineral cannot thank God for its creation
but man can do so in the name of the mineral. Man thus becomes the bridge between the realm of brute matter and the
realm of pure spirit. He is like unto matter inasmuch as he has
a body and like unto pure spirit inasmuch as he has a soul.
Standing midway between the two, he has been destined by
God to be the mouthpiece of creation and to chant with the
three youths in the fiery furnace a *Benedicite* to the Creator.
Such was Sacramentalism as the Scholastics conceived it and
as the Neo-Scholastics still conceive it. It is a system that looks
to the earth not as the forlorn hope of man but as the great
channel of spiritualization, and regards the tawdry tinsel of this
world's poor show as a stepping-stone to the tearless eternity
of the heavenly Jerusalem.

Philosophy in the Middle Ages was impersonal, dogmatic,
and sacramental. It was impersonal because truth was not the
property of an individual; it was sacramental because the world
was a stepping-stone to God. The art of this period was inspired by these thoughts and hence its three supreme characteristics are its impersonalism, its dogmatism, and its
Sacramentalism.

The impersonal and eternal note is struck in every phase of
the art of this period. Romances like the "Romance of the
Rose"; Latin hymns like the *"Dies Irae"* and those of the
"Little Hours," have come down to us with little or no trace of
the author who wrote them. The same must be said of the
works of art. The rose windows of the Cathedral of Lincoln,
pieces of which have come down to us, bear no trace of their
maker. None of the illuminated manuscripts of the Bible or the
missal or the breviary of this period are stamped with the name
of the artist. Since many of these works were made in cloisters,
it is likely that the rule of humility moved many of the artists to
hide their names. As a matter of fact, it is one of the rules of the
Benedictines that monks who work in monasteries shall produce works of art with great humility of spirit.

But the impersonal character is to be found in the Gothic

system, which, says Dr. De Wulf, "resembles Scholastic philosophy and helps us to understand it. For the Gothic system is the property of every one; while each architect may interpret it in his own way, it belongs in reality to no one. Even now, we do not kow the names of all those who conceived the plans and directed the work on the great cathedrals." And yet if our modern bridges and factories and smelting-plants survive four or five centuries, the generations of those days will know not only the name of the architect who designed them but even those of his assistants and the public officials of the time. Armies of sculptors chiseled the Virgins and the saints that occupy the portals and the niche, and yet how few of these have sealed their works with their names! The builders of the cathedrals, like Dante, were building for eternity; and in their minds, the materials of their structures were to survive for centuries; they were to last not for one generation but for all generations. Just as the thinkers of that time were hiding their identity because of the impersonality of truth and saying, *"Aliquis dicit,"* so too the artists of the time were hiding their identity in works of art that never betrayed the hand that held the chisel.

The reason of it all was that they were working for God. It mattered not for the mediaeval artist how obscure the portion of the cathedral at which he was set, he decorated it as beautifully as he knew how, without a thought that his work would be appreciated only by the few who would see it. Trivial details were finished with all the perfection of important parts. Microscopic studies in recent years have revealed beautiful designs of pollen-grains and diatoms that are far beneath the possibilities of human vision. Always these beauties were there, though hidden from the naked eye. Whether men saw these details, or the fineness of the technique, or the beauty of inspiration matters little. God saw, and that was enough. Hence it is not surprising to find statutes hidden in the tower of the Cathedral of Chartres that are just as perfect in detail as the statues above the door. Such impersonality in art could come only from a people who took a definite cognizance of the existence of God. The very silence of their work was an acknowledgment that their own artistry was from God and not from themselves. Why should their names be chiseled on stone when the gift of chiseling comes from God. Why should they cry out their own sufficiency when their whole being acknowledged their insufficiency? Why should they glorify themselves when only the glory of God mattered? Why should they care to leave their names to posterity as long as their names were written in the Book of Life?

And thus we have the superb spectacle of the Angel Choir of Lincoln, which is said to be the most beautiful work ever dropped from the hand of man, coming down to our own day without even a hint or a record of those who designed and executed it. Truly there was only one thing necessary—*unum necessarium*—the glory of God.

A dogma for the Middle Ages was a conceptual expression of an eternal religious truth. Unlike the modern world, those men did not believe that dogmas change like the styles of clothes. They are eternal, because they are truths about the eternal and immutable God. Being eternal, they could be put in stone—a lasting substance—so that the twentieth century, for example, could have that truth brought to it by the thirteenth, and testify to the thirteenth the indefectibility of dogma. If the mediaevalists had believed that dogmas were evolving they probably would have made their churches of gutta-percha, which could be fashioned to suit the whims of the changing centuries. The mediaevalists had more in common with the pagans of the past than with the neo-pagans of the present. It was Plato who said beautifully, over three centuries before the coming of Christ: "The artist who fixes his eyes upon the unchanging beauty and uses it as a model in reproducing the idea of virtue can never fail to produce a work of finished beauty, while he who has his eyes fixed on the changing things of time and their perishable models can make nothing beautiful." And Cicero tells us that Phidias "in making a Jupiter or a Minerva, did not have his eyes upon a particular model but upon a certain finished type of beauty which inspired his art and guided his hand." For all great artists dogmas of religion have been the inspiration of art. Religion is the foundation of art, says Rodin, and the essence of religion is dogma. The first poem is Genesis, the first architecture a Temple of God, and the first statue a deity. Like water rushing madly through narrow conduits that have no other outlet than from above, like the martys surrounded by the great hostile "thumbs-down" crowd of the Coliseum who had no means of escape but the open heavens above them, so too the soul cramped by the body seeks God as its outlet, pours out itself to Him to ravish itself with the ideal, to speak a language that enlightens, to carve and cut with the glorious liberty of the sons of God.

What are some of the dogmas that inspired the artists of those ages? If we are to judge by the works they have left us, any dogma sufficed to inspire them—the Trinity, the Incarnation, the Primacy of Peter, the Resurrection. From among them all we choose two that have been more or less forgotten or distorted by the modern age, namely Future Life as depicted by the Gospel, and the cult of the Blessed Virgin Mary.

The mediaevalists took the whole Gospel seriously and believed every word of it because they believed Him who gave testimony of the truth. When Christ said: "This is My Body, This is My Blood," they believed, and there was the dogma of the Eucharist. When Christ said to His Apostles and their successors: "Whose sins you shall forgive, they are forgiven them, and whose sins you shall retain, they are retained," they believed, and there was the dogma of Penance. When Christ said: "I am the Truth. . . . My Truth I give you," they believed, and there was the dogma of the Infallibility. When Christ said: "And the wicked shall be cast into everlasting fire with the devil and his angels," they believed, and there was the dogma of Eternal Hell.

The future life was something that was continually held up before the gaze of the mediaevalist. It was appointed unto all men once to die and after that the judgment. Death is frequently represented in the cathedrals and always with a fundamental optimism of making us reflect upon rather than fear death. In the beginning of the thirteenth century there flourished a poem that gave the key to much of the art of that period. It was called "The Dance of the Three Dead and the Three Living." Three young lords met one evening in the depths of an old cemetery. Three dead men appeared to them and each taught them a lesson: The first said, "I was Pope"; the second:

"I was a Cardinal"; and the third: "I was the secretary of the Pope." Then all three said: "Look on us now; you will be just as we are now, power, honors, and riches count for nothing. At the moment of death it is only good works that count." The story took on a slightly different form but still is easily recognizable in the window, "The Triumph of Death," at Campo Santo of Pisa. The "Danse Macabre" in the Cathedral of Amiens was likewise inspired by it; it embraces all human conditions from the king to the peasant. One of the most horrible reminders of death is the skeleton in the Church of St. Peter of Bar le Duc, which is covered with a film of half-rotted flesh hanging over the bones like a faded drapery. It is intended to produce a great feeling insecurity in this life even in the moments when we are most wedded to it.

The Last Judgement finds its best expression in the central door of the Cathedral of Notre Dame of Paris. Christ is seated in His Majesty showing the wounds of His hands; beside Him is the cross with which He has conquered death, and round about Him are the Blessed Virgin and angels. In a lower panel angels are going forth to the four corners of the earth and the utmost bounds of them with trumpets summoning the dead to rise to judgment. The just are signed with the Tau, the cross, and are placed on the right; the unjust are placed on the left and bound with ropes to be cast into utter darkness.

Heaven was represented as the heavenly Jerusalem descending from the sky, or else symbolically as the bosom of Abraham, such as we see it over the north door of Rheims Cathedral. Hell is represented by demons of hideous shapes, but best of all by a petrification of the words that Dante tell us are inscribed over hell, "All ye abandon hope who enter here." It was just such titanic glooms of the hopeless that inspired Fra Angelico's representation of Hell.

One of the favorite dogmas that inspired mediaeval art was the part of the Virgin Mary in the role of the redemption of the human race. It may be well to recall this dogma to those who are not familiar with it. There is a parallel between the Fall and the Redemption of man. Four elements contributed to the Fall: a disobedient man, Adam; a proud woman, Eve; a tree, and the fruit of the tree. Four elements contributed to our redemption:

An obedient God-man, Jesus Christ; a humble woman, the Virgin Mary; a tree, the Cross; and the fruit of the Tree, Christ and the Eucharist. As the human race fell through a woman it was fitting that it should be redeemed through a woman. Mary is more than a mere accident in the reparation of the human race, and is represented as something more, namely, as the Mother of God. Never is she depicted with a passing charm or a seducing femininity or as a fleshly thing that might be set to the music of Massenet, but always with the freshness and perfume and virginity of the Mother of God. On the west side of the Cathedral of Amiens there is a statue of her holding the Infant Who holds the world: under her feet is a devil being crushed by her heel, thus testifying that complete enmity would be placed between her and the devil, as foretold by Genesis—and acknowledged to-day in the dogma of the Immaculate Conception. Above the west door of the Cathedral of Paris there is a magnificent representation of her death and her coronation in Heaven, a subject that later on inspired Fra Angelico. In the Louvre hangs the famous painting wherein the Virgin is seated at the right hand of the Son in the triumph of her maternity. *"Astitit regina a dextris tuis, in vestitu deaurato."* In the center of the composition is Christ upon a throne, holding in both hands a crown, which He is placing on the head of His Mother. She kneels before Him, her hands folded across her breast. Around the throne are twenty-four angels singing her praises. Near them are saints of the Old and the New Testament, the very expression of whose visages testifies to the most pure and ineffable joy. Indeed Angelico understood what St. Thomas wrote of her beauty: "It purified the senses without in the least troubling them."

That this dogma of the Blessed Mother was once near and dear to the hearts of the mediaevalists, as it is to those who continue that tradition today, is evidenced by the number of churches dedicated in her honor. The Cathedral of Paris— Notre Dame—is one of the most glorious of these testimonials to Our Lady. Throughout the whole mediaeval empire and throughout England, cathedrals, shrines, and chapels were built in her name. In England there was such a devotion to her that England became known as "Mary's dowry" or "Mary's

England," which our modern world has corrupted to Merry England—as if it could be merry without Mary. And of all the sad visions that drop before a traveler in Europe today there are none more sad than ruins of the Lady chapels. During the English Reformation, and under the leadership of Cromwell, four hundred monasteries and churches were destroyed. Statues of the Blessed Virgin and other saints were reduced to dust by the hammers beating out a new civilization. The barren niches of Lincoln Cathedral, the decapitated statues of York, and the white-washed Lady chapel of Ely are so many sad vestiges today of that break with tradition.

In brief, the art of the Middle Ages is the art of a redeemed humanity. It is planted in the Christian soul at the border of living waters and under the Heaven of theological virtues and among the sweet zephyrs of the seven gifts of the Holy Ghost. For the Middle Ages there was no such thing as *making* Christian art. It was rather a matter of *being* a Christian. If you were a Christian, your art would be Christian. If you believed in eternal dogmas, your art would express eternal truth. Horace said, "If you wish me to weep, you must weep first," and the mediaevalist said, "If you wish to carve the things of Christ, you must live with Christ." Art for the mediaevalist demanded calm and meditation rather than hectic rush and excitement. History records that Fra Angelico wept while painting the "Crucifixion" that stands today in the Convent of San Marco in Florence.

The sacramental philosophy of the Middle Ages insisted that man is the center of the visible universe and that his life's mission is to lead creatures back to God. This Sacramentalism expressed itself in the art of the period, in making the cathedral the center of the political and social life of the time. Just as the religio-political life of the period converged towards the cathedral, so geographically the material structure of the city converged toward it. The Cathedral of Toledo, for example, is almost smothered by the structures that cling around it. It was foreign to the mind of the mediaevalist to set the church off at a distance as if to magnify its beauty. Like to a mother who is surrounded by her children, who frolic like sheep about her, so too the cathedral welcomed the homes and drew them to her bosom. It was not distant and fearful admiration it solicited, but confidence and love. Like a mighty ocean greyhound ready for its voyage, the whole city seemed to embark within its flanks.

Just as the cathedral was the center of the political and social life of the time, so the Real Presence was the center and soul of the cathedral. As man, the microcosm, summed up all visible creation within himself, whose vital principle was a soul, so too the cathedral summed up all creation within itself, and its soul was the Eucharistic Emmanuel. The world is a great sacrament and the cathedral is a still greater one. The cathedral synthetized everything. All kingdoms, the mineral, the vegetable, the animal, the human, and the angelic—all arts, all sciences, all times—left their trace on it. All nature rebelled with Adam and all nature was redeemed with Christ. Hence Our Lord, when he sent out His Apostles to teach, did not say "Preach the Gospel to every man," but "Preach the Gospel to every creature." The architects of the cathedrals again took Him at His word and brought every creature into their structures; there are trees and flowers and birds and fishes. There are statues of cows on the top of the Cathedral of Laon, and vegetables over the door of the Cathedral of Rheims.

And the principle that unified these things, what was it? Not a city like Mecca; not an organ or a pulpit, but God amongst men—not the mere abstract Great Architect of the Universe, nor a pantheistic equation with the world, but God mysteriously living under the appearance of Bread. There is a real heart palpitating in this sacramental universe of the cathedral and that heart is the Sacred Heart in the real sacrament of the Eucharist. This Divine Life bound together like a hoop of steel the various hierarchies of creation found therein. It did more than that; it revealed to the worshipers that great procession of life—Divine Life—that passes from Father to Son in the Trinity, from Son to human nature in the Incarnation, and from the Incarnation to us in the Eucharist, and which finally, to complete the circle, is some day to lead us back to God. "All are yours, you are Christ's, and Christ is God's." The Gothic cathedral, which is the philosophy of the Middle Ages in stone—can we ever forget it?

"Far away and long ere we catch the first view of the city itself," says Reinach, "the three spires of the Cathedral, rising above the din and turmoil, preach to us the Most High and Undivided Trinity. As we approach, the transepts striking out crosswise tell us of the Atonement. The Communion of Saints is set forth by the chapels clustering around the choirs and nave: the mythical weathercock bids us to watch and pray and endure hardness; the hideous forms that are seen hurrying from the eaves speak the misery of those who are cast out of the church; spire, pinnacle, and finial, the upward curl of the sculptured foliage, the upward spring of the flying buttresses, the sharp rise of the window arch, the high-thrown pitch of the roof, all these overpowering the horizontal tendency of string course and parapet, teach us that vanquishing earthly desires, we also should ascend in mind and heart. Lessons of holy wisdom are written in the delicate tracery of the windows; the unity of many members is shadowed forth by the multiplex arcade; the duty of letting our light shine before men, by the pierced and lowered parapet that crowns the whole."

We enter. The triple breadth of the nave and aisles, the triple height of pier-arch, triforium, and clerestory, the triple length of choir, transepts, and nave, again set forth the HOLY TRINITY. And what besides is there that does not tell of our Blessed Saviour, that does not point out HIM FIRST in the western door; HIM LAST in the distant altar; HIM MIDST in the great rood; HIM WITHOUT END in the monogram carved on boss and corbel, in the Holy Lamb, in the Lion of the Tribe of Judah, in the mystic Fish? Close by us is the font, for by regeneration we enter the Church; it is deep and capacious, for we are buried in Baptism with CHRIST; it is of stone, for He is the rock; and its spiry cover teaches us, if we be indeed risen from its waters with Him, to seek those things which are above. Before us in long-drawn vista are the massy piers, which are the Apostles and Prophets—they are each of many members, for many are the graces in every saint; there is beautiful delicate foliage around the head of all, for all were plentiful in good works. Beneath our feet are the badges of worldly pomp and glory, the graves of kings and nobles and knights— all in the presence of God as dross and worthlessness. Through the walls wind the narrow cloister galleries, emblems of the path by which the Church's holy monks and anchorites, whose conflicts were known only to their God, have reached their home. And we are compassed about with a mighty cloud of witnesses; the rich deep glass of the windows teems with saintly forms, each in its own fair niche, all invested with the same holy repose; there are the glorious company of the Apostles, the goodly fellowship of the Prophets, the noble army of martyrs, the shining band of confessors, the jubilant chorus of virgins. There are kings who have long since changed an earthly for a heavenly crown, and bishops who have given in a glad account to the Shepherd and Bishop of souls. But on none of these things do we rest; piers, arch behind arch; windows, light behind light; arcades, shaft behind shaft; the roof, bay behind bay; the saints around us; the Heavenly Hierarchy above with dignity and pre-eminence still increasing eastward—each and all lead eye and soul and thought to the image of the Crucified Saviour as it glows in the great east window. Gazing steadfastly on, we pass up the nave, that is, through the Church Militant, till we reach the rood-screen, the barrier between it and the Church Triumphant, and therein shadowing forth the death of the faithful. High above it hangs on His triumphant CROSS the image of HIM Who by His death hath overcome death; on it are portrayed saints and martyrs, His warriors, who fighting under their Lord have entered into rest and inherit a tearless eternity. They are to be our examples, and the seven lamps above them typify those graces of the SPIRIT by Whom alone we can tread in their steps. The screen itself glows with gold and crimson; with crimson, for they passed the Red Sea of martyrdom to obtain them. And through the delicate network, and the unfolding holy doors, we catch faint glimpses of the chancel beyond. There are the massy stalls, for in Heaven is everlasting rest; there are the sedilia, emblems of the seats of the Elders round the Throne; there is the piscina, for they have washed their robes and made them white; and there, heart and soul and life of all, the altar with its unquenchable lights, and golden carvings, and mystic steps, and sparkling jewels; even CHRIST Himself, by whose merits only we find admission to our heavenly inheritance.

† 14 †

A Declaration of Dependence

There has never been an anti-American movement in the United States that did not, in one form or another, appeal to the Declaration of Independence. Communists base their right to destroy democracy on the Declaration of Independence; monopolistic capitalists invoke it to escape even a just government supervision for the common good; the so-called Progressive educators appeal to it to mold children independently of religion; spurious defenders of civil liberties tearfully quote it to justify every attack upon the foundations of liberty; in a word, the Declaration of Independence has come to mean for a group of our fellow citizens nothing other than independence of authority, law, and order.

In these days when everyone talks of rights and few of duties, it is important for us Americans to recall that the Declaration of Independence is also a Declaration of Dependence. The Declaration of Independence asserts a double dependence: dependence on God, and dependence on law as derived from God.

Where do we get our right of free speech? Where do we get freedom of conscience? Whence is derived the right to own

139

property? Do we get these rights and liberties from the State? If we did, the State could take them away. Do we get them from the Federal Government in Washington? If we did, the Federal Government could take them away. Whence comes the right to life, liberty, and the pursuit of happiness?

Read the Declaration of Independence and there find the answer: "We hold these truths to be self-evident, that all men are created equal, that they are *endowed by their Creator* with certain unalienable Rights, that among these are Life, Liberty and the pursuit of Happiness." Notice these words: *The Creator has endowed men with rights and liberties;* men got them from God! In other words, we are dependent *on God,* and that initial dependence is the foundation of our independence.

Suppose we interpret independence, as some liberal jurists do, as independence of God; then rights and liberties come either from the State, as Bolshevism contends, or from the Dictators, as Nazism and Fascism believe. But if the State or the Dictator is the creator of rights, then the State or the Dictator can dispossess men of their rights. That is why in those countries where God is most denied, man is most enslaved. It is only because we are dependent on God that we are independent as persons from the total will of any man on earth.

Let us not think that by denying God we will have purchased independence. The pendulum of the clock that wanted to be free from its point of suspension, found that on becoming independent of its suspension, it was no longer free to swing. The Communists and the Nazis and the Fascists who denied God as the source of their freedom got in the end the inglorious freedom of State prisoners.

Democracy is based not on the Divine Right of Kings but on the Divine Right of Persons. Each person has a value because God made him, not because the State recognizes him. The day we adopt in our democracy the already widespread ideas of some American jurists that right and justice depend on convention and the spirit of the times, we shall write the death warrant of our independence. When watchmakers set watches according to their whims and not according to a fixed point of reference, such as the sun, we will no longer have the right time;

when aviators build machines in repudiation of the laws of gravitation, we will no longer fly; and when we deny God as the foundation of our rights, we shall no longer have rights. The Declaration of Independence, I repeat, is a Declaration of Dependence. We are independent of dictators because we are dependent on God.

Because we are dependent on God, it follows that it is religion's first duty to preserve that relationship between man and his Creator. Religion and democracy, therefore, are not the same. Some religious leaders never once in their discourses mention the name of God, but actually define religion as democracy. Certain alarmists, when a personal representative of the President was sent to the Holy Father, shrieked against union of Church and State—but they do not protest against the identification of religion and democracy, which is an insult to both religion and democracy. If religion is democracy, then let us drop religion and become State servants; if democracy is religion, then let us scrap democracy and enter a monastery. Religion is not democracy. The two are as different as man's soul, and democracy is primarily for the prosperity and common good of the nation. God is not Caesar and Caesar is not God. Have our so-called religious leaders forgotten: "Render therefore to Caesar the things that are Caesar's; and to God, the things that are God's?"

Once religion abdicates its soul-saving mission as its primary end, it becomes as ridiculous as mathematicians turned theologians. There is too much of an interchange between professions. We think that because a man is an expert in one field he is an expert in all. Because Einstein knows the relativity of space and time, some think that he should therefore be regarded as an authority on God. This is as incongruous as that a theologian should be consulted as an expert on space and time. Both of them would be talking about something neither of them know anything about. There should be standards for all professions. A barber, in order to get a license, must know how to cut hair; a plumber must know how to thread pipe; a stonecutter must know how to chisel—in the right sense of the term. But in the field of religion it is too commonly assumed that a man can be an authority without being religious. A minimum condition that should be imposed upon all who talk religion is that they say their prayers.

The primary service of religion is not to preserve a democracy identical with our own, for if it were, there could be no religion where there was a method of government different from our own. The primary business of religion is God; to bring man to God and God to man. Religion's service to democracy is secondary and indirect; that is, by concentrating on spiritualizing the souls of men, it will diffuse through political society an increased service of justice and charity rooted in God.

There is no such thing as saving democracy alone. Democracy is a branch, not a root. The root of democracy is the recognition of the value of a person as a creature of God. To save democracy alone is like saving the false teeth of a drowning man. First save the man and you will save his teeth. First preserve belief in God as the source of rights and liberties and you will save democracy. But not vice versa. Religion's greatest contribution to democracy is by serving something else. Just as a man loves a woman best on condition that he loves virtue more, so religion serves democracy best when it loves God most all: "Seek ye therefore first the kingdom of God, and his justice, and all these things shall be added unto you."

Too long have men taught that God must serve democracy; it is now time to affirm the contrary. Democracy should serve religion—likewise indirectly, of course, in the sense that it will be obedient to a justice born of God and not of expediency; that it will give equal economic opportunities to all, provide the normal comforts of life, guarantee employment, in order that citizens being freed from economic or political injustices will be free to serve their God. Democracy serves religion indirectly by removing those obstacles and disadvantages which stand in the way of man achieving the more glorious liberty of the children of God. As Washington told us: ". . . let us with caution indulge the supposition that morality can be maintained without religion. Whatever may be conceded to the influence of refined education or minds of peculiar structure, reason and experience both forbid us to expect that national morality can prevail in exclusion of religious principles.''

Not only does the Declaration of Independence affirm dependence on God, it also affirms dependence on law. After saying that our rights came from God, this historic document adds: ''. . . to secure these rights, Governments are instituted among Men, deriving their just powers from the consent of the governed.'' This means that all men come to the State with rights antecedent and independent of the State, because so endowed by God. Persons so divinely endowed transfer this authority to a ruler whom they designate, or in the words of the Declaration of Independence: ''Governments derive their just powers from the consent of the governed.'' But what interests us now is that governments so instituted have as their mission to secure and preserve rights and liberties given by God. In other words, we are dependent *on the authority of a good government for the preservation of our rights.* Authority exists to preserve freedom. This needs to be stressed because there is too general a tendency in our country today to interpret freedom as absence of law and restraint; there are even those who would oppose liberty and law by defining freedom as the right to do whatever you please. There are certain groups and organizations in this country that will defend you if you evade the draft, slap a teacher, teach immorality to students, hiss the President, or do anything contrary to law and justice. Their defense of your anarchy will be in the name of liberty. They talk about freedom as if it were an end in itself, a life rather than an atmosphere of life. That is why they never tell us what we are going to do *with* freedom. They forget that freedom *from* something, implies freedom *for* something, as this story illustrates: A liberal one day went up to a taxi driver and said: ''Are you free?'' The taxi driver who hadn't had a job in two days said: ''Yes, I'm free.'' The Liberal left shouting: ''Hurrah for freedom!'' In just such a plain way as this our modern leaders are leaving us up in the air about freedom. Freedom from all dependence, such as dependence on God, dependence on law, dependence on truth, is not independence—it is the beginning of slavery. Freedom, it must be reaffirmed, is not a physical power, but a moral power. Of course, you can do anything you please, you can shoot your neighbor's chickens and stuff your mother's mattress with razor blades. You *can* do these things, but *ought* you! Freedom is a *moral* power; not a *physical* power; not the right to do what you *please*, but the right to do whatever you *ought*. But *ought* implies law, and law implies order, and order implies justice, and justice implies God.

There are two classes of citizens in the United States: those who interpret the Declaration of Independence as meaning independence of God and independence of law; and those who hold that we are independent because we believe in God as the root of law and believe in law as the ground of freedom. We Catholics belong to the second group. There are many others, cutting across all religious classes, who believe similarly. And to them we appeal to save true Americanism by social and national affirmation of our dependence on God, particularly in these days of national conscription. Our government after due debate and consideration of national danger has ordered national conscription. Therefore we accept it as the law of the land. But what would happen if, while assenting to it, we did not as a nation declare our dependence on God? The point is that mobilization of man power on the part of the State could be very dangerous if it were not compensated for by a deepened religious sense of dependence on God.

This is easy to understand. There are many cohesions and groupings to which men belong that are not exclusive and possessive. For example, a man who belongs to an athletic club is not excluded from joining the Plumbers Union or a Bridge Club. But there is one grouping which is much more exclusive and that is the nation; a citizen of one country cannot be a citizen of another. Because a nation is by its nature exclusive of other nations and other peoples, it is very easy for it to become exclusive of all other loyalties, including God. The mobilization of man power which may indeed be very desirable if we are in danger of attack, would be fraught with evil if at the same time men did not affirm their dependence on God.

Suppose in a crisis such as this, we forgot our Declaration of Dependence; suppose we forgot there was no higher community of men than the State; suppose that, in a day when the State claims the body, we failed to affirm that our souls are our own by offering them to God—it would not be long until the State, seeing that we recognized nothing else but the State, could claim us body and soul. Thus while organizing to combat the totalitarian evil abroad we would become its victims at home.

That is why it is particularly important for us as a nation to reaffirm our allegiance to another community, namely, the brotherhood of men under the Fatherhood of God. The more and more unified we become in an army, the greater the need that we declare our obligation to God from whom we derive our inalienable rights and to whose Divine Providence we have entrusted this nation. It is illuminating to observe that in every State in the modern world where there has been universal conscription *to the exclusion of God,* there has been erected a slave state.

By a national act of adoration and petition we can prevent conscription of man power from becoming conscription of man; by it we affirm that the army is not the whole of life. In the clear language of St. Thomas in his commentary on the Politics of Aristotle, we must remember that "man belongs to the community, but not according to the whole of his being." He belongs to the community as an individual, because he is part of a whole; but he does not belong to the community as a person endowed with an immortal soul, for the spirit can be a part of nothing. Man belongs to the army as regards his *function,* but not as regards his *inalienable rights* which comes to him from God. Man in his military service is not, like a plant eaten by an animal, wholly transformed into the Moloch of the State. There is within him something the State cannot possess, namely, his soul. But unless citizens take cognizance of the fact that they have souls by declaring their loyalty to God, the State may say: "Since you profess no other allegiance than to us, then you belong wholly to us." That is totalitarianism— man totally, body and soul, belonging to the State.

Be not deceived by slogans about democracy, as if it were like an heirloom which once possessed needs only to be preserved. Democracy is an endowment like life, and needs to be repurchased in each new generation. Democracy is not the luxury of civilization; it is not affluence which obscures injustice by the comparative comfort of the oppressed; it is not a license which allows freedom to be destroyed by invoking rights without duties. Christianity has a new battle before it; it is no longer with scorn that calls itself Skepticism; no longer with dilettantism which masquerades as Learning; no longer with injustice which called itself Progress—but with the new pride which would free governments from the moral restraints of God and authority. In the hour that is dawning the Church must defend democracy not only from those who enslave it from without, but even from those who would betray it from within. And the enemy from within is he who teaches that freedom of speech, *habeas corpus,* freedom of press, and academic freedom, constitute the essence of democracy. They do not. They are merely the accompaniments and safeguards of democracy. Given a freedom which is independent of God, independent of the moral law, independent of inalienable rights as the endowment of the Divine Spirit, America could vote itself out of democracy tomorrow. How can we continue to be free unless we keep the traditions, the grounds, and the roots upon which freedom is founded? We could not call our soul our own unless God exists. Why, we would not even have a soul! Democracy has within itself no inherent guarantees of freedom; these guarantees are from without. That is why I say our Declaration of Dependence on God is the condition of a Declaration of Independence of Dictatorship. The greatest defenders of America are not necessarily those who talk most about freedom and democracy; it is the sick who talk most about health. For that reason there should be less loose talk about democracy and freedom; instead of judging religion by it attitude toward democracy we should begin to judge democracy by its attitude toward religion. For in a crisis such as this America will save her Stars and Stripes by grounding them on other stars and stripes than those which are on the flag, namely, the stars and stripes of Christ, by whose stars we have been illumined and by whose stripes we have been healed.

† 15 †

The Emergence of Morals

Evil in the world seems to be an argument against the Power, Righteousness, and Justice of God, but it is only seems. *Evil is one of the consequences of a moral universe where freedom reigns, and where characters emerge by the right use of freedom.*

If God is power, love, and justice, then why did He create this kind of world? If He is powerful, why does He permit evil? If He is love, why does He tolerate hate? If He is justice, why does He allow unrighteousness? These questions, I suppose, have been asked by everyone whose eyes have ever seen, whose minds have ever known the terrible contrast between the sin of the world and the goodness of God.

In order to answer correctly the question why God made this kind of world, it is important, first of all, to remember that this is not the only kind of world that God could have made. He might have created ten thousand other kinds of worlds, in which there never would have been struggle, pain, or sacrifice. But this is the best possible kind that God could have made for the purpose He has in mind. An artist is to be judged not so much by the masterpiece he produces, as by the purpose he had in mind in creating the masterpiece. An architect is not to be judged a poor architect because he designs a bird house instead of a cathedral, for his intention may have been only to construct a haven for the winged creatures of God instead of a dwelling for God Himself. In like manner, God must not be judged only by this particular kind of world which He created, but also by the intention and will He had in making it.

This brings us to the other question: What purpose did God have in mind in making this kind of world? The answer is very simply that God intended to construct a moral universe. He willed from all eternity to build a stage on which characters would emerge. He might, of course, have made a world without morality, without virtue, without character—a world in which each and every one of us would sprout virtues as an acorn sprouts an oak, or a world in which each of us would become saints with the same inexorable necessity that the chariot of the sun mounts the morning sky, or the rain falls to embrace the earth. God might have made us all like so many sticks and stones, in which we would be guided by the same necessity by which fire is hot and ice is cold. God might have done this, but He did not. And He did not because He willed a moral universe in order that, by the right use of the gift of freedom, characters might emerge. What does God care for things, piled into the infinity of space, even though they be diamonds, for if all the orbits of heaven were so many jewels glittering like the sun, what would their external but necessarily undisturbed balance mean to Him in comparison with a single character, which could weave the skeins of an apparently wrecked and ruined life into the beautiful tapestry of saintliness and holiness? The choice before God in creating the world lay between creating a purely mechanical universe, peopled by mere automata, or creating a world of pure spiritual beings, for whom the choice of good and evil was, at any rate, a possibility.

Suppose, now, it be granted that God chose to make a moral universe, or one in which characters would emerge. What condition would have to be fulfilled in order to make morality possible? If God chose to make a moral universe, then He had to make man free; that is, endow him with the power to say "yes" and "no," and to be captain and master of his own fate and destiny. Morality implies responsibility and duty, but these can exist only on condition of freedom. Stones have no morals, because they are not free. We do not praise iron because it becomes heated by fire, nor do we condemn ice because it is melted by heat. Praise and blame can be bestowed only on those who are masters of their own will. It is only the man who has the possibility of saying "no" who can have so much charm in his heart when he says "yes." Take this quality of freedom away from a man, and it is no more possible for him to be virtuous than it is for the blade of grass which we tread beneath our feet. Take freedom away from life and there would be no more reason to honor the fortitude of the martyrs who offered their bodies as incense in testimony of their faith, than the honor the flames which kindled their faggots. Take away liberty and where would be the concern in how children will mold their lives and write their eternal destiny in the invisible ink of their free choice. Take away freedom which gives life the interest of an everlasting plot, and with how little care would we watch the curtain rise, and with what feeble regret would we watch the drop scene fall.

Is it any impeachment of God that He chose not to reign over an empire of chemicals? If, therefore, God has deliberately chosen a kind of empire not to be ruled by force but by freedom, and if we find His subjects able to act against His will, as stars and atoms cannot, does this not prove that He has possibly given to them the chance of breaking allegiance, in order that there may be meaning and glory in that allegiance when they freely choose to give it?

We have said that God chose to make a moral universe, and secondly, that He could make a moral universe only on condition that He made man free. This being so, we have an answer to the question, why does God permit evil? The possibility of evil is in some way bound up with the freedom of man. Since man was free to love, he was free to hate; since he was free to obey, he was free to rebel; since he was free enough to be praised for his goodness, he was free enough to be blamed for his badness. Virtue, in this present concrete order, is possible only in those spheres in which it is possible to be vicious; sacrifice is possible only in those levels in which it is possible to be selfish; redemption is possible only in those realms where it is possible to be enslaved. The world has no heroes except in those battles where every hero might have been a coward; the nation has no patriots except in those causes where each patriot might have been a traitor; the Church has no saints except in those realms where each heart might have been a devil. Triumphal arches are reared only to men who succeeded, but who might have failed in the trying; niches are filled only by the statues of those who might have transgressed, but did not; monuments are erected only to the memory of those who might have turned back, and yet pushed on.

Take the danger and doubt away from life, and where would be the heroism and faith? Let there be no sorrow by night, no malady by day, and where would be kindness and sacrifice? No watchful love hovers over the invulnerable; no crown of merit ever rests suspended over those who do not fight; they might all go forth to battle and enterprise alone, and be forgotten, followed by no musing fancy that is flushed with their triumph, or anguished with their fall. A world without contingency could have no hero or no saint. There is no epic of the certainties, and no lyric without the suspense of sorrow and the sigh of fear, and there can be no morality in the present order without the possibility of evil, and no saints without the possibility of each one becoming a Judas.

If, then, the possibility of evil is in some way involved in human freedom, one can immediately see the absurdity of condemning God for allowing evil to continue. How many there are who say, "If I were God, I would immediately destroy all injustices and evils." To ask this, however, is to ask that God contradict Himself; you ask that God should create a thing free to choose between good and evil, and yet oblige that thing to choose good. To ask that God should create a man free to choose between justice and injustice, and yet oblige him always to choose justice and never be unjust, is to ask an absurdity. Just as it is impossible in the very nature of things for God to create me and not to create me, to make me exist and not exist at the same time, so it is impossible in the nature of things for God to make me free and yet to make me a slave. God cannot do anything which would contradict His nature, not in the sense the He is bound by anything outside Himself, but because His nature is justice itself.

And so those who would blame God for allowing man freedom to go on hindering and thwarting His work, are like those who, seeing the blots and smudges and misspellings and grammatical errors in a student's notebook, would condemn the teacher for not snatching away the book and doing the copy himself. Just as the object of the teacher is sound education and not the production of a neat and well-written copybook, so the object of God is the development of souls and not the production of biological entities, however perfect they may be. There, too, is the answer to those who ask: "If God knew that I would sin why did He make me?" Very simply, insofar as I am a sinful being, God did not make me. I made myself. I am a self-creating being. God gave me power, but I am free to decide the manner of man I shall be. Hence my success or failure is in my own hands and I am responsible for the result.

Since the universe is moral, it follows that the supreme choice which lies before us is that of obeying the law of God, or rebelling against it. If you choose to rebel against that law as though you were your own, and as if Christ had never bought you with His Blood, then you must remain eternally in the congregation of the dead. Not for you will be the glory of consecrated knowledge, not for you the rich blessings of Him who turns a soul from the error of its ways; not for you the steady love of good, though it be persecuted, or the steady scorn of evil, even though it be enthroned; but for you the frivolous insipidity of unreverent amusements—the dull and discontented mind, ignoble when with another, wretched when alone. Great deeds will be done, but you will not be at their doing; high thoughts will be uttered, but they shall awaken no echo in the seared conscience and sodden heart. Beyond you shall sweep the Godlike procession of the nobly virtuous and the greatly wise, but you shall not be found among their ranks. If you choose to offend God, successful you may be, honored you may be, rich you may be, praised by the world you may be, "broad-minded" and "progressive" you may be, alive to public opinion and to the new morals of the day you may be, but you will never know how much you have failed, as Barabbas never knew how much he failed the day of his success. But you will be dead! dead to the life of Christ! dead to the love of God! dead to the ageless peacefulness of eternity!

If, on the contrary, you obey the laws of God and live as if you were really destined for a life beyond the grave, the battle in which the love of God gains mastery over the love of self may be fierce, and for the short time of our bodily life every tree may be a cross, every bush may be a crown of thorns, and every friend may be a Judas. Poor you may be on this earth, with no more comfort than a Carpenter once had at Nazareth, sorrowful you may be as each day brings to you a new cup of passion, filled with the bitterness of Gethsemane; solitary you may be with not even a Veronica to wipe away the salt of righteous tears; scorned and ridiculed you may be by a world of darkness that comprehends not the light; thirsty you may be as your soul, in the fire of its crucifixion, cries out for the cool draughts of a Divine Refreshment; a failure you may be, an unworldly dreamer, a fool, but in all the world's burnt wilderness your food shall be the Manna from the Paradise of God, and your drink the fountain of everlasting life. But alive you shall be, alive to Christ! alive to the spirit! alive to life! alive to God! and if God is your life, then who can take it from you?

† 16 †

The Purifying Flames

Three possible states await a soul after death: a state of perfect Love without suffering which is heaven; a state of suffering without Love which is Hell, and a state of Love with suffering which is Purgatory. Purgatory is the creation of the Mercy of God.

There is one word which to modern ears probably signifies the unreal, the fictional and even the absurd in the Christian vision of life, and that is the word *purgatory*. Although the Christian world believed in it for sixteen centuries, for the last three hundred years it has ceased to be a belief outside the Church, and has been regarded as a mere product of the imagination, rather than as a fruit of sound reason and inspiration. It is quite true to say that the belief in purgatory has declined in just the proportion that modern mind forgot the two most important things in the world: the Purity of God and the heinousness of sin. Once both of these vital beliefs are admitted, the doctrine of purgatory is unescapable. For what is purgatory but a place or condition of temporal punishment for those who depart this life in God's grace, but are not entirely free from venial faults or have not entirely paid the satisfaction due to their transgressions? In simpler language, love without suffering is heaven; suffering without love is hell; and suffering with love is purgatory. Purgatory is that place in which the love of God tempers the justice of God, and secondly, where the love of man tempers the injustice of man.

First, purgatory is where the love of God tempers the justice of God. The necessity of purgatory is grounded upon the absolute purity of God. In the Book of the Apocalypse we read of the great beauty of His City, of the pure gold, with its walls of jasper and its spotless light which is not of the sun nor moon but the light of the Lamb slain from the beginning of the world. We also learn of the condition of entering the gates of that heavenly Jerusalem: "There shall not enter into it anything defiled, or that worketh abomination, or maketh a lie, but they that are written in the book of the life of the Lamb." Justice demands that nothing unclean, but only the pure of heart shall stand before the face of a pure God. If there were no purgatory, then the Justice of God would be too terrible for words, for who are they who would dare assert themselves pure enough and spotless enough to stand before the Immaculate Lamb of God? The martyrs who sprinkled the sands of the Coliseum with their blood in testimony of their faith? Most certainly! The missionaries like Paul who spend themselves and are spent for the spread of the Gospel? Most assuredly! The cloistered saints who in the quiet calm of a voluntary Calvary become martyrs without recognition? Most truly! But these are glorious exceptions. How many millions there are who die with their souls stained with venial sin, who have known evil, and by their strong resolve have drawn from it only to carry with them the weakness of their past as a leaden weight.

The day we were baptized, the Church laid upon us a white garment with the injunction: "Receive this white garment which mayest thou carry without stain before the judgment seat of our Lord Jesus Christ that thou mayest have life everlasting." How many of us during life have kept that garment unspotted and unsoiled by sin so that we might enter immediately upon death into the white robed army of the King? How many souls departing this life have the courage to say that they left it without any undue attachment to creatures and that they were never guilty of a wasted talent, a slight cupidity, and uncharitable deed, a neglect of holy inspiration or even an idle word for which every one of us must render an account? How many souls there are gathered in at the deathbed, like late-season flowers, that are absolved from sins, but not from the debt of their sins? Take any of our national heroes, whose names we venerate and whose deeds we emulate. Would any Englishman or American who knew something of the purity of God, as much as he loves and respects the virtues of a Lord Nelson or a George Washington, really believe that either of them at death were free enough from slight faults to enter immediately into the presence of God? Why the very nationalism of a Nelson or a Washington, which made them both heroes in war, might in a way make them suspect of being unsuited the second after death for that true internationalism of heaven, where there is neither English, nor American, Jew nor Greek, Barbarian nor Free, but all one in Christ Jesus our Lord.

All these souls who die with some love of God possessing them are beautiful souls, but if there be no purgatory, then because of their slight imperfections they must be rejected without pity by Divine Justice. Take away purgatory, and God could not pardon so easily, for will an act of contrition at the edge of the tomb atone for thirty years of sinning? Take away purgatory and the infinite Justice of God would have to reject from heaven those who resolve to pay their debts, but have not yet paid the last farthing. Purgatory is where the love of God tempers the justice of God, for there God pardons because He has time to retouch these souls with His Cross, to recut them with the chisel of suffering, that they might fit into the great spiritual edifice of the heavenly Jerusalem, to plunge them into that purifying place where they might wash their stained baptismal robes to be fit to enter into the spotless purity of heaven; to resurrect them like the Phoenix of old from the ashes of their own suffering so that, like wounded eagles healed by the magic touch of God's cleansing flames, they might mount heavenward to the city of the pure where Christ is King and Mary is Queen, for, regardless of how trivial the fault, God cannot pardon without tears, and there are no tears in heaven.

On the other hand, purgatory is a place not only where the love of God tempers the justice of God, but where the love of man may temper the injustice of man. Most men and women are quite unconscious of the injustice, the ingratitude, and the thanklessness of their lives until the cold hand of death is laid upon one that they love. It is then, and only then, that they realize (and oh, with what regret!) the haunting poverty of their love and kindness. One of the reasons why the bitterest of tears are shed over graves is because of words left unsaid and deeds left undone. "The child never knew how much I loved her." "He never knew how much he meant to me." Such words are the poisoned arrows which cruel death shoots at our hearts from the door of every sepulcher. Oh, then we realize how differently we would have acted if only the departed one could come back again. Tears are shed in vain before eyes which cannot see; caresses are offered without response to arms that cannot embrace, and sighs stir not a heart whose ear is deaf. Oh, then the anguish for not offering the flowers before death had come and for not sprinkling the incense while the beloved was still alive and for not speaking the kind words that now must die on the very air they cleave. Oh, the sorrow at the thought that we cannot atone for the stinted affection we gave them, for the light answers we returned to their pleading and for the lack of reverence we showed to one who was perhaps the dearest thing that God had ever given us to know. Alas, too late! It does little good to water last year's crop, to share the bird that has flown, or to gather the rose that has withered and died.

Purgatory is a place where the Love of God tempers the Justice of God, but also where the love of man tempers the injustice of man, for it enables hearts who are left behind to break the barriers of time and death, to convert unspoken words into prayers, unburned incense into sacrifice, unoffered flowers into alms, and undone acts of kindness into help for eternal life. Take away purgatory and how bitter would be our grief for our unkindnesses and how piercing our sorrow for our forgetfulness. Take away purgatory and how meaningless are our memorial and armistice days, when we venerate the memory of our dead. Take away purgatory and how empty are our wreaths, our bowed heads, our moments of silence. But, if there be a purgatory, then immediately the bowed head gives way to bent knee, the moment of silence to a moment of prayer, and the fading wreath to the abiding offering of the sacrifice of that great Hero of Heroes, Christ.

Purgatory, then, enables us to atone for our ingratitude because through our prayers, mortifications, and sacrifices, it makes it possible to bring joy and consolation to the ones we love. Love is stronger than death and hence there should be love for those who have gone before us. We are the offspring of their life, the gathered fruit of their labor, the solicitude of their hearts. Shall death cut off our gratitude, shall the grave stop our love, shall the cold clod prevent the atoning of our ingratitude? The Church assures us that not being able to give more to them in this world, since they are not of it, we can still seek them out in the hands of Divine Justice and give them the assurance of our love, and the purchasing price of their redemption.

Just as the man who dies in debt has the maledictions of his creditors following him to the grave, but may have his good name respected and revered by the labor of his son who pays the last penny, so too the soul of a friend who has gone to death owing a debt of penance to God may have it remitted by us who are left behind, by minting the gold of daily actions in the spiritual coin which purchases redemption. Into the crucibles of God these departed souls go like stained gold to have their dross burned away by the flames of love. These souls, who have not died in enmity with God, but have fallen wounded on the battlefield of life fighting for the victory of His cause, have not the strength to bind their own wounds and heal their own scars: it remains for us who are still strong and healthy, clad with the armor of faith and the shield of salvation, to heal their wounds and make them whole that they might join the ranks of the victors and march in the procession of the conquerors. We may be sure that if the penny that gives bread to the hungry body delivers a soul to the table of our Lord, it will never forget us when it enters into the homeland of victory.

While yet confined to that prison of purifying fire, they hear the voices of the angels and saints who call them to their true fatherland, but they are incapable of breaking their chains for their time of merit is passed. Certainly God cannot be unmindful of a wife who offers her merits to the captive soul of a husband waiting for his deliverance. Surely the mercy of God cannot be such that He should be deaf to the good works of a mother who offers them for the liberation of her offspring who are yet stained with the sins of the world. Surely God will not forbid such communication of the living with the dead, since the great act of Redemption is founded on the reversibility of merits. Responsive, then, will we be to the plea not only of our relatives and friends but of that great mass of unarmed warriors of the Church Suffering who are yet wearing the ragged remnants of sin, but who, in their anxiety of soul to be clothes in the royal robes fit for entrance into the palace of the King, cry out to our responsive hearts the plaintive and tender plea: "Have mercy on me, have mercy on me, at least you, my friends, for the hand of the Lord has touched me."

† 17 †

The Fact of Hell

Love forgives everything except the refusal to Love, and Hell exists for those who refuse to love Love. The absence of Love is one of its greatest punishments.

If there is any subject which is offensive to modern sentimentalists it is the subject of hell. Our generation clamors for what the poet has called "a soft dean, who never mentions hell to ears polite," and our unsouled age wants a Christianity watered so as to make the Gospel of Christ nothing more than a gentle doctrine of good will, a social program of economic betterment, and a mild scheme of progressive idealism.

There are many reasons why the modern world has ceased to believe in hell, among which we may mention, first a psychological reason. If a man has led a very wicked life, he does not want to be disturbed in his wrongdoings by harsh words about justice. His wish that there be no final punishment for his crimes thus becomes father to the thought that there is no such thing as hell. That is why the wicked man denies hell, whereas the saint never denies it only but fears it.

Another reason for the denial of hell is that some minds confuse the crude imagery of poets and painters with the reality of the moral order behind the doctrine. Eternal realities are not always easy to portray in the symbols of time and space, but that is no reason why they should be denied by anyone, any more than the reality of America should be denied because it is sometimes symbolized by a woman bearing a flag of red, white, and blue.

A final reason is found in the reason that the doctrine of hell has been isolated from the organic whole of Christian truths. Once it is separated from the doctrines of sin, freedom, virtue, redemption, and justice, it becomes as absurd as an eye separated from the body. The justice of this reasoning is borne out in the fact that men become scandalized about hell when they cease to be scandalized about sin. The Church has never altered one single iota the belief in an eternal hell as taught by her Founder, our Lord and Saviour, Jesus Christ. In adherence to His divine testimony, the Church teaches, first that hell is a demand of Justice, and secondly, that hell is a demand of Love.

First of all, once it is recognized that the moral order is grounded on justice, then retribution beyond the grave becomes a necessity. All peoples have held it morally intolerable that by the mere fact of dying, a murderer or an impenitent wrongdoer should triumphantly escape justice. The same fate cannot lie in store for the martyr and the persecutor, Nero and Paul, the Judas and Christ. If there is a supreme Good to which man can attain only by courageous effort, it must follow that the man who neglects to make that effort imperils his felicity. Once it is granted that eternal life is a thing which has to be won, then there must always be the grim possibility that it may also be lost.

Even the order of nature itself suggests retribution for every violation of a law. There is a physical law to the effect that for every action there is a contrary and equal reaction. If, for example, I stretch a rubber band three inches, it will react with a force equal to three inches. If I stretch it six inches, it will react with a force equal to six inches. If I stretch it twelve inches, it will react with a force equal to a foot. This physical law has its counterpart in the moral order, in which every sin necessarily implies punishment. What is sin but an action against a certain order? There are three orders against which a man may sin: first, the order of individual conscience; secondly, the order of the union of consciences, or the State; and thirdly, the source of both, or God. Now, if I sin or act against my conscience, there is a necessary reaction in the form of remorse of conscience which, in normal individuals, varies with the gravity of the sin committed. Secondly, if I act or sin against the union of consciences or the State, there is a contrary and equal reaction which takes the form of a fine, imprisonment, or death sentence meted out by the State. It is worthy of note that the punishment is never determined by the length of time required to commit the crime, but rather by the nature of the crime itself. It takes only a second to commit murder, and yet the State will take away life for such an offense. Finally, whenever I sin against God, and this I do when I rebel either against the order of conscience or State, I am acting contrary to One who is infinite. For this action, there is bound to be a reaction. The reaction from the Infinite must, therefore, be infinite, and an infinite reaction from God is an infinite separation from God, and an infinite separation from God is an eternal divorce from Life and Truth and Love, and an eternal divorce from Life and Truth and Love is—*hell!*

It should be evident, therefore, that eternal punishment is not an arbitrary construction of theologians, but is the very counterpart of sin. We are too often wont to look upon hell as an afterthought in the mind of God and regard it as related to sin in the same way that a spanking is related to an act of disobedience on the part of a child. This is not true. The punishment of spanking is something which does not necessarily follow upon an act of disobedience. It may be a consequence, but it need not be. Rather it is true to say that hell is related to a sinful and evil life in the same way that blindness is related to the plucking out of an eye, for the two are inseparable. One necessarily follows the other. Life is a harvest and we reap what we sow: if we sow in sin, we reap corruption; but if we sow in the spirit, we reap life everlasting.

The teaching of our Blessed Lord bears out this demand of

justice, for His doctrine was not merely an amiable gospel of indifference on His own life was not one of sentimental good-naturedness. He very distinctly taught that men might do things which would prove their undoing. Never did He give assurance that He would succeed with everyone. The very fact that He poured out His life's blood to redeem us from sin could only mean that sin might have such a terrible consequence as hell. For, on the last day, the good shall be separated from the bad, and the sheep from the goats. Then "shall the King say to them that shall be on His right hand: Come, ye blessed of My Father, possess you the kingdom prepared for you from the foundation of the world. For I was hungry, and you gave Me to eat: I was thirsty, and you gave Me drink: I was a stranger, and you took Me in. . . . Amen, I say to you, as long as you did it to one of these My least brethren, you did it to Me. Then He shall say to them also that shall be on His left hand: Depart from Me, you cursed, into everlasting fire which was prepared for the devil and his angels. For I was hungry, and you gave Me not to eat: I was thirsty, and you gave Me not to drink. I was a stranger, and you took Me not in. . . . As long as you did it not to one of these least, neither did you do it to Me. And these shall go into everlasting punishment: But the just, into life everlasting." These are the words of the Son of God who is Truth Itself, and it is difficult to understand why anyone, knowing and admitting this, should accept His words concerning heaven, and deny His words concerning hell. If He is worthy of belief in one instance, He must be worthy of belief in another.

Not only is hell demanded by justice, but also by love. The failure to look upon hell as involving love makes men ask the question, "how can a God of love create a place of everlasting punishment?" This is like asking why a God of Love should be a God of Justice. It forgets that the sun which warms so gently may also wither, and the rain which nourishes so tenderly may also rot. Those who cannot reconcile the God of Love with hell do not know the meaning of love. There is nothing sweeter than love; there is nothing more bitter than love; there is nothing which so much unites souls and so much separates them as love. Love demands reciprocity; love seeks a lover; and when love finds reciprocity, there is a fusion and a compenetration and a union to a sublime and ecstatic degree. And when it is a question of the love of God and the love of the soul, that is, the happiness of heaven. But suppose that love does not find reciprocity; or suppose that love does find it only to be betrayed, spurned, and rejected. Can love still forgive? Love can forgive injuries and betrayals and insults, and Divine Love can forgive even to seventy times seven. But there is only one thing in the world which human love cannot forgive, and there is only one thing in eternity which Divine Love cannot forgive, and that is the refusal to love. When, therefore, the soul by a final free act refuses to return human love for Divine Love, then Divine Love abandons it to its own selfishness, to its own solitariness, to its own loneliness. And what punishment in all the world is comparable to being abandoned, not by the lovely but by the Love which is God?

Love forgives everything except one thing, and that is the refusal to love. A human heart pursues another and sues for its affection with all the purity and high ardor of its being. It showers the loved one with gifts, tokens of sacrifice, and all the while remains most worthy of a responding affection. But if, after a long and weary pursuit, it has not only been spurned and rejected and betrayed, that human heart turns away and bursting with a pent-up emotion in obedience to the law of love, cries out: "Love has done all that it can. I can forgive anything except the refusal to love."

Something of this kind takes place in the spiritual order. God is the Great Lover on the quest of His spouse, which is the human soul. He showers it with gifts, admits it into His royal family in the sacrament of baptism, into His royal army in the sacrament of confirmation, and invites it to His royal table in the sacrament of the Everlasting Bread, and countless times during human life whispers to it in health and sickness, in sorrow and joy, to respond to His plaintive pleadings, abandon a life of sin, and return love for love. If, however, the human heart, after rejecting this love many times only to be reloved again, after ignoring the knock of Christ at the door of his soul only to hear the knock again, finally, at the moment of death

† 18 †

The New Taboo

What adds to loneliness and diminishes the joy of the *pneuma* is the new taboo. In the Victorian days it was sex. A discreet silence was kept on anything that had to do with birth, generation, and the carnal expression of love. That taboo has been done away with, though its elimination has not diminished problems associated with it, as was claimed. What is the taboo of the twentieth century which corresponds to the nineteenth-century taboo on sex? The taboo of death.

In the more Christian days, death was something that was always kept in mind and for which we were to be prepared: *Memento mori.* Now the physicians shrink from telling the patient that he is dying, that he might prepare for it either legally or spiritually. Patients are sometimes kept alive with a network of tubes from oxygen tanks long after consciousness has departed. Besides depriving a person of his death through silence, there is an awkwardness in the face of death itself. Mourners do not know what to say to the bereaved. Preachers are instructed not to refer to it but rather to gardens, fresh flowers, and gentle winds blowing through meadows.

The same evasions that were told in the Victorian days about sex—namely, the stork bringing babies—are told today about death. Funeral cosmetics are used to destroy that borderline between life and death; mourning, widows' weeds, black bands, plumed horses, elaborate hearses, all conspire to cover up the inevitable. Even when it is spoken of, it is covered up with words such as: "It has to come to all of us," or "Everyone must die."

Bruce Marshall in his novel, *Fair Bride,* writes:

> Down in the street, the municipal hearse flashed by on one of its daily journeys to the cemetery. From the high window the naked corpse lying in the unlidded coffin looked like a doll in a cardboard box. There were no mourners and no priests. There was no hope, no despair, no mystery. Everything was simple and clear: life meant something only because it meant nothing.

Tennessee Williams in *Camino Real* makes the last receptacle of our outworn humanity not the graveyard, but the garbage pail.

This taboo on death has brought on what might be called the Second Fall, when understanding of immortality is lost. Perhaps now we have reached an age when we may speak of the two falls or two types of humanity. The once-fallen had hope in the Redeemer; the twice-fallen live in a universe that is silent, where radar sends back no sound, where the center of the universe has fallen apart, and belief in future life has vanished. One is asked to be brave when life is meaningless. This is what is called "heroism with its eyes out," as Carlyle described the ethics of John Stuart Mill. The humanity of the Second Fall is disillusioned with nature, with humanity, and with society; nothing makes sense. The only point of death is its absurdity. Karl Marx once described belief in life after death as "pie in the sky." In the Second Fall, there is neither a pie nor a sky. Camus expressed it well for the Second Fall: "There is but one truly serious philosophical problem and that is suicide." Why stay alive in a meaningless universe? In that meaningless universe, he died as he crashed his car into a tree.

Some grow old physiologically while they attempt to remain young psychologically. They try to stop the clock of life, or else to turn the hands back, hugging to childhood. Sexagenarians put on rouge, imagining themselves to be in their teens; they are as pillars of salt, fixed in their flight from death, with no close bond either as the youth which they seek to imitate or to the living reality of their present hour.

The Reason for the Taboo

In previous ages, men lived in existence at which there were two ends, neither of which belonged to existence itself. One was birth, the other death. Birth and death were the two questions which made one ask: "Where did I come from?" "Where am I going?"

Birth itself was not explicable by existence, for it was before my existence. Otherwise we would have to say that the egg was the cause of the chicken which laid it. Death, too, is not explicable by our existence, for it is its negation. Suppose now one cuts off these two terminal points of birth and death from existence—then life becomes meaningless. As long as men pondered about their origin and their destiny, neither of which were explicable by their finiteness, they could find answers to the riddle of life. But once these great questions were no longer pondered, the universe ceased to be transparent like a window; it became opaque like a curtain. The sacred was written off as the unreal, and one did his best to settle down to a kind of cosmic coziness which was never very cozy. The old became afraid to die, the young afraid to live.

What we cannot explain we disavow and ignore. The time span of life becomes meaningless, since it was without an origin and a destiny, as a journey is meaningless without a point of departure and a point of arrival. The subject of death thus became a taboo in which there was a disavowal of death through face-lifting, the refusal to recognize one's age, the denial of responsibility, the glorification of the absurd, and fondness for death songs among the youth. Playwrights came to the rescue by staging, as Ionesco did, a corpse which gradually rose until it floated away as a balloon to nowhere. The periodical injection of paraffin into the corpse of Lenin is the Communist way of avoiding the taboo of death and giving immortality, which it denies, to mortality.

Despite the disavowals, there are some psychologists who deplore "the slick, smooth operation of easing the corpse out by saying no to weeping, wailing, and expressing grief and loneliness. What effect does this have psychologically? It may mean that we have to mourn covertly, by subterfuge—perhaps in varying degrees of depression, perhaps in mad flights of activity, perhaps in booze." Another psychologist recalls that it might result in "a callousness, a rational preoccupation with the fear of death and vandalism."

Decades of Communism have not hidden the desire for something beyond the temporal. In *Dr. Zhivago*, the work suppressed by the Communists, Boris Pasternak writes: "It was not until after the coming of Christ that time and man could breathe freely. It was not until after Him that men began to live toward the future. Man does not die in the ditch like a dog—but at home in history, while the work called the conquest of death is in full swing; he dies sharing in this work."

Psychiatry

The psychiatrist best equipped to deal with this subject is a Jew who himself saw tens of thousands of his people, as well as Christians, go to the awful furnaces of Auschwitz and other concentration camps. Only he who lived with death knows anything about it. Dr. Viktor Frankl writes in *From Death Camp to Existentialism* that psychological observations of thousands of prisoners revealed that men who let go of the inner hold of their moral and spiritual selves generally fell victim to the degenerating influence of the camp. But what was this "inner hold"? It was "a goal to reach." The man who lacked this inner hold generally fell into retrospective thoughts, contrasting his early experience with those of the present, and thus fell into a blue mood. Dr. Frankl then further defines this inner hold:

It is a peculiarity of man that he can only live by looking to the future—*sub specie aeternitatis*.

. . . The prison who had lost his faith in the future was doomed. . . . Some prisoners had dreams that on a certain day they would be released. They immediately picked up in the light of that illusion. But when they were not released on that day, they died almost immediately. As Nietzsche has said: "He who has a *why* to live for can bear with almost any *how*."

One woman told the doctor that she was grateful that life had hit her so hard, for in her preprison days she had wasted her opportunities and ignored her spiritual development. Now, she said, "I am happy, for I have a tree out there in my loneliness. And that tree speaks to me every day, and it says to me: 'I am eternal life.' "

Another prisoner made a pact with Heaven that his suffering and death should save the human being that he had loved the most. He did not want to die for nothing. What threatens man is an existential vacuum or nothing to live for. What gives him hope is something in the future to which he can dedicate his life. Then "the sufferings of this life are not worthy to be compared to the joys which are to come."

When anyone gave up the future, he said: "I had nothing more to expect from life." In prison, as long as men were living for a future, such as a wife and children or a home or medical books to write, they were sustained in the present.

If a temporal future so much sustains, how much more strength was given when the future was a goal? As a result of living so close to death, Dr. Frankl, out of his prison experience, developed what he called logotherapy—man is not dominated by the will to pleasure not by the will to power but by the *will to meaning*. Without this, man suffers an existential void. He then began to put into practice a lesson from the Talmud: "Whoever destroys even a single soul should be considered the same as man who destroyed the whole world. And whoever saves even one single soul is to be considered the same as the man who has saved a whole world." The saving of the soul is giving them not just a hope for the future, but a goal and a destiny.

In contrast, Ernest Hemingway wrote of the crash of 1929 when men who adored money lost their "god":

> Some made the long drop from the apartment or the office window; some took it quietly in the two-car garage with the motor running; some used the native tradition of the Colt or Smith and Wesson; those well constructed weapons which end insomnia, terminate remorse, cure cancer, avoid bankruptcy, blast an exit from intolerable positions by the pressure of a finger; those admirable American instruments so easily carried, so sure of effect, so well designed to end the American dream when it becomes a nightmare, their only drawback is the mess they leave for relatives to clean up.
> —ERNEST HEMINGWAY, *To Have and Have Not*

In another work he wrote:

> "Last week the old man tried to commit suicide," the old waiter said.
> "Why?" asked the second waiter.
> "He was in despair."
> "What about?"
> "Nothing."
> "How do you know it was nothing?"
> "He has plenty of money."
> —ERNEST HEMINGWAY, *A Clean, Well-Lighted Place*

The thought of the future makes it possible to bear some of the trials of life. Imagine a child who is given a ball to play with. He is told that it is the only ball that he will ever have in his life. The natural effect will be that he will be afraid to play with it too much, afraid to lose it, afraid of its wearing out—the thought of ultimate dissolution will be a constant harrassment to him, even when he bounces and throws it.

But suppose that he is told that maybe next year or maybe in five years, but sometime in the not-too-distant future, he will be given another ball which will never wear out and which will give him happiness the like of which he has never before known. The natural reaction of the child will be not to be too much concerned with the first ball, because he is going to have another. The belief in the future world sustains the trials of this, for thus one fits meaning into the universe.

Freud holds that every one psychologically has a belief in the future, inasmuch as he is a spectator to his death.

We have tried to keep a deadly silence about death. After all, we even have a proverb to the effect that "one thinks about something beyond, as one thinks about death." After all, one's own death is beyond imagining, and whenever we try to imagine it, we can see that we really survive as spectators. Thus the dictum should be dared in the psychoanalytic school: at bottom, nobody believes in his own death. Or, and this is the same: in his unconscious everyone is convinced of his own immortality.

The Law of Death in Nature's Life

Every mortal has both an outer and an inner life. The outer life is his reaction to environment, his wealth, his amusement, and his pleasures. His inner life is his character, his spirit, his motivation, his heart. Man is very much like a barrel of apples. The apples that are seen on the top are his reputation, but the apples down below represent his character.

It is a law of life that while the "outer man begins to grow older, the inner man is often renewed from day to day." The spirit can grow, while the body is decaying. How often the beauty of the inner life appears even amidst the decrepitude of a perishing body. Milton lost his sight, but his poetic vision increased.

A man is very much like a plant. Divinely endowed with one impulse that tends to push him out into the world, he has also a companion impulse that inclines him to the earth. If a plant were conscious, there might be a danger that it would throw all of its vigor into the roots or that it might concentrate wholly on the bloom and fruit. This would be to forget that in the realm of matter, as well as in spirit, all laws are twins. Each one is balanced by an opposite. The visible must be balanced with the invisible, the material with the spiritual, the love of God with the love of neighbor on earth. Man is two worlds at one and the same time.

Because man is rooted in both the physical and the spiritual, it is possible for him to share in the evolutionary process and to undergo the transformation that he finds in nature. One basic law running through all nature is that no realm ever enters into a higher one, without death to that which is lower. This process has been called the catabolic. Plant life says to the carbons, the phosphates, the sunshine, the rain, and all the chemicals about it, "Unless you die to yourself, you cannot live in my kingdom." Only if you surrender your lower form of existence in the chemical order, will you begin to be a part of the kingdom of vibrating vegetable life.

If the animals could speak, they would say to the plants and to the chemicals: "Unless you die to your lower existence, you cannot live in my kingdom." But if you surrender yourself, mortify your lower existence, you will become a part of sentient life, a feeling, seeing, moving creature. Man, in his turn, speaks to the chemicals, the plants and animals and says, "If you will die to your lower existence, if you consent to be plucked up by the roots, commit yourself to knife and fire, and even to the shedding of blood, you will live in my kingdom—you will be a part of a thinking being that can know the stars, write poetry, and even take a trip to the moon."

This law of immolation in the lower order is not voluntary, simply because the lower orders are not either conscious or endowed with reason. But in virtue of their immolation, they do not cease to be what they are—chemicals, plants, and animal life—but they are transformed and elevated, reborn and ennobled in a higher life.

This evolution of the universe should not stop with man. He has no right to say there is no higher life above him, any more than a rose has a right to say there is no life about it. Certainly there should be some nature, some kingdom above man into which he can be assumed, in order that his nature might be reborn. The law that would operate would be the same—he would have to die to his lower nature before he could live in the Divine. Nothing is born to a higher life, unless it be born from above. Chemicals would not be born into plants unless there was a higher life to take them up. Animals would not be born into man unless there was human life to assume them. Man cannot be reborn unless there is the kingdom above him. "Unless the grain of wheat fall into the ground and die, it remains alone." God would first have to come down to man, and man in his turn would freely have to consent to be taken up in the Divine order. The lower kingdoms are seized; man is free, he must consent. The tragedy of life is not what men suffer but how much they miss by refusing to follow the evolution of the universe. What is struggle for existence in nature becomes sacrifice and self-denial for man.

Could we but crush that ever-craving lust
for bliss, which kills all bliss; and lose our life,
Our barren unit life, to find again
A thousand lives in those for whom we die:
So were we men and women, and should hold
Our rightful place in God's great universe,
Wherein in heaven and earth, by will and nature,
Nought lives for self. All, all, from crown to footstool
The lamb, before the world's foundation slain,
The angels, ministers to God's elect;
The sun, who only shines to light a world;
The clouds, whose glory is to die in showers;
The fleeting streams who in their ocean graves
Flee the decay of stagnant self-content;
The oak, ennobled by the shipwright's axe;
The soil, which yields its marrow to the flower;
The flower which breeds a thousand velvet worms,
Born only to be prey to every bird—
All spend themselves on others; and shall man,
Whose twofold being is the mystic knot
Which couples earth and heaven—doubly bound,
As being both worm and angel, to that service
By which both worms and angels hold their lives—

Shall he, whose very breath is debt on debt,
Refuse, forsooth, to see what God has made him?
No, let him show himself the creature's lord
By free-will gift of that self-sacrifice
Which they, perforce, by nature's law must suffer;
Take up his cross and follow Christ the Lord.

The power to find life through death makes the seed nobler than the diamond. In falling to the ground it loses its outer envelope which is a restraining power of the life within it. But once this outer skin dies, then life pushes forth into the blade. So, too, unless we die to the world with its vices and its concupiscences, we shall not spring forth into life everlasting. If we are to live in a higher life, we must die to the lower life. If we live in the higher life of Christ, we must die to the lower life of egotism.

To put the whole law in the beautiful paradox of Our Divine Lord: "If you wish to save your life you must lose it"; that is, if we wish to save it for eternity, we must lose it for time. If we wish to save it for the Father's mansions, we must lose it for this dull world. If we wish to save it for perfect happiness, we must lose it for fleeting pleasure of mortality. The transformation of nature through death, which is the law of evolution, cannot exist everywhere in nature, except in man. This upward surge, this progress toward greater perfection must be allowed to man as well as to fish, only it must respect his freedom. Once granted a thorough evolution, death is the doorway to life. Then all the trivial mortifications of life become rehearsal for the ultimate self-denial of death, which opens the seed to Resurrection and Life.

The fall doth pass the rise in worth;
For birth hath in itself the germ of death
But death hath in itself the germ of birth
It is the falling acorn buds the tree,
The falling rain that bears the greenery,
The fern plants moulder when the ferns arise.
For there is nothing lives but something dies,
And there is nothing dies but something lives,

Till the skies be fugitives,
Till Time, the hidden root of change, updries
Are Birth and Death inseparable on earth;
For they are twain yet one, and Death is Birth.
                    —FRANCIS THOMPSON

When the struggle for existence in the physical order becomes self-denial of pride, lust, avarice in the psychic order,
one sees that death is the prelude to a higher life. In man this
might be called excentration—he moves out of himself as
center, to another Center Who has obeyed the same Law by
undergoing a Good Friday for the sake of an Easter Sunday.

Death is My-ness

Every man must do certain things for himself; blow his own
nose, make his own love, do his own sleeping, and die his own
death. Heidegger added, "Dying is something that nobody can
do for another." In Vienna there is a sardonic saying: "So
many people now die who never died before." This means they
are undergoing a form of "self-denial" which they never practiced before. La Rochefoucauld said, "One can no more stead-
ily look at death than at the sun." But he forgot that by looking
at the sun, we begin to understand its mysteries. It is thanks to
the inability to look at the sun that we see everything else
under the sun. As Chesterton said, "We can see the moon and
things under the moon, but the moon is the mother of luna-
tics."

Man differs from all other creatures, inasmuch as he knows
that *he will die.* Out of the present he orients himself to the
future. Even nature has something of this, for out of any chemical facts a scientist is able to predict future combinations.

Could it not be that our attitude toward death is very much
what our attitude would have been to birth, had we been conscious? Would we not have shrunk back just as much from the
portals of birth as we do now to the portals of death? Is not a
beginning either in time or eternity the cause of an equal reluc-
tance? There is only One Who has ever made such an affirma-

tion of preexistence. When Our Lord was reproached, saying He was not yet fifty years old, His answer, as casual as a man looking over his shoulder, was, "Before Abraham was, I am." He did not say, "Before Abraham was, I was." He speaks of a beginning from all eternity and not the uncounted billions of years, but the very principle of life itself.

Because death is something every man must go through, it is not a problem but a mystery. A problem is something we see from the outside; a mystery must be seen from the inside. A problem is mere objectivity, such as how to send a rocket to the moon. A mystery is a participation and a sharing in the problem itself. Imagine three men holding a copy of Shakespeare's soliloquy of Hamlet, "To Be or Not to Be." One cannot read, though he sees all the letters just as well as any reader. The second can read, but he knows nothing about Shakespeare or the plot of the play. The third is so familiar with the background of the soliloquy that, when he reads it, he transcends it and sees in it the mystery of existence and nonexistence. We are so used to science and technology that the only information we consider as valid is that which comes unrelated to ourselves, something which we approach from the outside, rather than something into which we are submerged. What cannot be investigated as a scientific problem, we are apt to ignore as unreal, forgetful that much technological knowledge is based on substitution, such as the airplane for the train; while a profounder knowledge is based on the deepening of a mystery, such as comes to husband and wife in marriage.

Death is not a problem but a mystery, inasmuch as it personally concerns me, however much I may seek to avoid it. What heightens its mystery is not only that it will happen to me, but that neither I nor any one else has direct experience of it. It cannot be experienced from without. Each and every one has to undergo it himself.

The only answer to the mystery of death would be for someone to break the death barrier, as we have broken the sound barrier, so that, as sound and fury are left behind in speed, so death would be left behind in the newness of life. Someone must pierce the mystery from within. Man could lift his hands in protest against heaven, unless in some way God tasted death. How often a mother, before she gives medicine to a child, takes it herself and says, "See! Mother does not mind." Should not God also take His own medicine, namely, Death?

God Takes His Own Medicine

On Good Friday men announced, "God is dead." They set watches, they sealed a tomb, and they signed the death certificate. There had to be a moment like this—when it was absolutely certain God was dead—before an ultimate reason could be given to the mystery. The skepticism should be greatest, not among the unbelievers but among believers—the kind of people who accepted death as final, so final that they would bring spices to anoint the body, impugn witnesses who would say He was alive, and shrug them off, saying, "A woman's tale." Never was the world so close to brightness and the solving of the riddle of death as when learned professors, lawyers, and scribes of temples of philosophy trumpeted, "God is dead!" This fact had to be first before there could be hope.

The veil of the mystery could be lifted only by the most persistent and convinced of all the God-Is-Dead-ers—the type of man who would absolutely refuse to believe those who saw the empty tomb and the Conqueror of Death in the transformed glorious state of the Victor. That skeptic, whose name was Thomas, would have to give to future generations the one test: "I am not going to believe anything beyond death, until I can apply the same test I apply to men who say they have been to war. What care I if they wear medals on their breasts—these can be bought! I want to see the marks inflicted by the God-Is-Dead crew; I want proof that He has been to war against death. What proof is in an unscarred hero who says he has been in a shell hole or a ditch? Let me see the place where the God-Is-Dead-ers drove in nails, bayonet wounds when they pierced His side, the Feet so dug with steel that He had to be carried off the battlefield on a stretcher. Once I see these scars of One Who battled death and conquered, then—and then only—shall I believe.''

When this President of the Society of God-Is-Dead-ers throws himself prostrate before Him, saying, ''My Lord and My God''—I will believe. Then, my faith rests not on just the testimony of those who saw Him, but in the response of the scientist who probed Hands, Feet, and Side to bring to final conviction that He Who was dead lives.

There is no other answer to the riddle of death. Philosophies and world religions can never enlighten the mystery until someone crashes the impregnable wall. And when that Death was preceded by poverty, hunger, thirst, hatred, miscarriage of justice, intellectual barbarism, and scourgings, and the seeming abandonment of heaven and flies that could not be brushed away from a bleeding, crown-pierced Head, then I know that nothing that happens to me or anyone else can be worse and that it is eventually to be swallowed up in joy and peace.

From that day to this, we say to Him Who stumbled to His Throne, ''How can You allow polio to strike down a child, cancer still the hand of a musician, and death lay its cold hand on a young mother.''

And Christ answers, ''Can you not see that everything that touched you first touched Me; that every tightening of a violin string is not for the sake of pain but to give a richer melody, that every stroke of a hammer on the marble is not to punish stone but to bring out the beautiful form hidden therein? I am in the midst of your sorrows; your tears run down My cheeks; your thirst is but an echo of My parched cry of the Cross. Every demon I drove out leered at Me; I died the very death that I conquered. Who among you fears death, and I did not fear? Who among you dies, and I did not die with you? In fact, I am the First Born from the Dead. Suffering and death are hostile powers. You struggle against them. So did I. But everything that strikes you first struck Me. It had to pass through My Hands before it touched your hands. No greater truth was ever announced on this earth than 'God is dead.' Once you know this you are on the road to the next chaper of the Book: 'He

Who is dead is now alive. See the place where they laid Him.' "

The Resurrection

Just suppose a man is put on trial for murder, the evidence against him being complete except for the fact that the body of the murdered man was not discovered. All the evidence that was brought out in court revealed the exact time of the murder, the testimony of hundreds who saw it, the instruments of torture used in the crime, and the official documentation of police, military, and religious authorities.

Suppose that immediately after the judge had sentenced the guilty man to death, the one who was murdered walked into the courtroom alive! The judge would have to say that the *corpus delicti* was a living man. How dare accuse one of murder when the murdered is living? There would be nothing to do but to release the condemned man.

Something of this kind is present in the man of faith who believes in the Resurrection. His guilt is beyond dispute; he has even confessed it. His rebellion was heartless; his sin indelible. But at that point, where he shamefully admits to crucifixion, lo and behold! the Crucified appears not only alive but as Life. The trial is over. All his sins are swallowed up by faith in the Resurrected Man Who brings forgiveness.

Hence there are two ways of facing death. One is the way of the pessimistic existentialist whose novels, poetry, and plays resolve around the one theme: Find a lonely man, tell him that he is under the threat of death, and he will be more lonely than he was before. He will make a philosophy out of his loneliness, ridicule his friends and his neighbors who are afraid to face up to the fact that they will die; he himself will always have it before his face. He invites it; he scorns it. He boasts that it clears his head. He stands on the edge of precipices, on the railings of bridges and of ships, spitting in the face of death. He calls everyone else a coward who is afraid to face death in this absurd life.

The Christian has always faced death but not with such morbidity. He makes a rehearsal for death by many acts of self-denial: "I die daily," and, "I am crucified with Christ." His mortification is a daily death, a kind of preparation for the ultimate.

The existentialist dies for his own sake, and the Christian dies for Christ's sake. One is centered in self-consciousness, and the other is centered in Other-consciousness.

Hammer and the anvil, the potter and the clay, the sculptor and the stone, the surgeon and the ulcer, the gold and the fire—out of the hammering and the beating and the purging and the flame something takes shape. But in order that it might do it, there must be some kind of cooperation. As Augustine put it: "Without God, we cannot; without us, He will not."

Behind the transformation is love—love for God Who was Dead. This fact became the basis of a story by Tolstoy, *The Death of Ivan Ilyich*. Ivan, as well as all the other members of his family and his group, uses the expression that "one dies" without ever personally relating it to himself. There is, however, one in the group, a poor servant, who knows that he has to die, and he turns to changing the attitude of Ivan, bringing great love to bear upon him. Ivan begins to see that what is important is not so much that he is dying of a diseased kidney, but that his life has been pointless, wasted, frustrated, and to no purpose. Under the impact of love, he then begins to care for others, to feel sorry, and for the three days preceding his death he keeps repeating, "Life! What joy!"

Love, therefore, has a double effect on the attitude toward death. First, it changes our sense of values and turns blessings into curses and curses into blessings. It does this through a sense of forgiveness. Secondly, it changes the selfishness of life into service, as it did with Ivan Ilyich. One of the supreme examples of turning the blessing into a curse was the thief on the right, to whom pain was the worst of all evils except impending death. Then suddenly, the light flashes, and he asks to be taken into Paradise, to which there comes the answer: "This day." And the thief died a thief because he stole Paradise.

Finally, in *The Brothers Karmazov* by Dostoyevsky, we have the whole story of how we come to the solution of the mystery, where we hear the anguished cry of a woman:

> Life beyond the grave . . . what a tremendous puzzle. The mere thought of it shakes me to the point of anguish, torment, and even terror. . . . Do I live only to disappear without a trace, except for the weeds growing on my grave, as some writer said? It is a terrifying outlook. What shall I do? What am I supposed to do, in order to recapture my faith! . . . As a child I accepted faith spontaneously without question. . . . But how shall I go about finding the truth now? Where am I to look for the proofs? Not a soul, in fact, hardly anyone in this world today, seems to be concerned with these things. Yet, I myself cannot bear the burden of my own ignorance. It is a terrible feeling.

Father Zozima answers her question. No doubt, this is a terrible nightmare. No one can really prove these things. And yet, it is possible for us to convince ourselves of their truth. . . . But how? Through the experience of active love. Try to love your neighbor with relentless, active affective fervor. As your love grows, you will become more and more convinced of both the existence of God and the immortality of the soul. And if your love for yourself reaches the heights of complete mystery, there will be no doubt left. This is a sure, proven way.

† 19 †

Collective Life-Collective Death

The world is the scene not only of cultural differences, economic inequalities, the subjects of previous chapters; here we shall consider the great problem of the survival of the world itself.

According to Teilhard de Chardin, the evolution of the universe through millions of years has seen the gradual unfolding of a proto-consciousness, until man appeared as fully conscious and rational. But within the last thirty thousand years, he holds there has been no radical change either on the somatic or on the mind level of man. One thing for him is certain: Man's development does not lie in the begetting of some superman; evolution in that direction has practically ceased. From now on, progress, instead of being vertical, will be horizontal—that is, will reach out to the unification of all mankind.

In the earlier phases, the complex atoms entered into new unities and eventually produced a form of life. When one comes to the animal kingdom, one finds socialization, while the higher one goes in the progression of humanity, the more one finds that individuals become less and less isolated, more and more socialized. Psychology reveals also that individuals reach a higher state of perfection in community than they do when separated from a community. As Teilhard puts it: "No evolutionary future awaits man except in association with other men."

Thanks to communications, education, global network of trade and exchange, men and nations are weaving a pattern of greater and greater interdependence. This vast globality of common effort is what Teilhard calls the noösphere. Humanity is now at the crossroads of collective life or collective death. If it is to survive, what energy was to the lower order love must be the human—namely, the drive to more and more complex social unity. Teilhard opts for collective life. The birth of mankind is a consequence of the birth of man. Borderlines between nations and cultures will gradually be effaced. Peoples will see more and more that they cannot live in isolation and that they must associate with one another.

At this point one can see a slight parallel between the thinking of Karl Marx and Teilhard de Chardin. Both thought the world was developing toward socialization. Marx believed that the socialization would be a kind of ant heap in which the individual lives only for the mass, resulting in a complete loss and submerging of personality. Teilhard de Chardin felt that the socialization would result in an increase of freedom for personality. As he put it: "A tremendous spiritual power is slumbering in the depths of our multitude, which will manifest itself only when we have learned to break down the barriers of our egoisms."

This is possible, because both at the beginning and at the end of the whole evolutionary process, there is Love. The Love-point at the beginning which makes everything turn from complexity to unity is the Alpha; the goal toward which all tends is the perfect Love or the Omega. As he wrote:

> One day the Gospel tells us, the tension gradually accumulating between humanity and God will touch the limits prescribed by the possibilities of the world. And then will come the end. Then the Presence of Christ, which has been silently accruing in things will suddenly be revealed—like a flash of light from pole to pole.
>
> —*The Divine Milieu*

Collective Death

An opposite view to Chardin's is that there will be a socialization which will produce a Superman and eventually end in the destruction of humanity. The mass society which will be formed will destroy personality. As Lenin wrote: "The whole society will be one office and one factory with the same work and the same wages." Lenin called the leader of this mass society the "dictatorship of the proletariat." Friedrich von Preen, in the same spirit, held that the great future authority was developing toward an absolute center of power. Our Blessed Lord spoke of such a one as the "Prince of this world," St. Paul called him "the god of this world" (II Cor. 4:4). St. John called him "an other" and said, "If an other comes in his own name, him will you receive" (John 5:43). It is to be noted that when Satan in the temptations offers Christ all of the kingdom of the world and the glory thereof, saying, "For to me they have been delivered, and whomever I will I give them" (Luke 4:6), Christ does not correct him.

Christopher Dawson, sees the world as entering "into a new phase of our culture in which the most amazing perfection of scientific technique is being devoted to purely ephemeral objects . . . it is obvious that a civilization of this kind holds no promise for the future, save that of social disintegration."

The Spaniard, Donoso Cortes, in 1849 wrote: "Mankind is hastening with great strides towards the certain fate of despotism . . . this despotism will evolve a power of destruction greater and mightier than anything we have hitherto experienced."

Dostoyevsky makes Ivan Karamazov say:

"As soon as men have, all of them, pronounced that God is dead, man will be lifted up with a spirit of the divine, titanic pride, and the man-god will appear. . . . Man will unite to take from life all that it can give for nothing else but for the joy and happiness in the present world."

The new collectivity, effected through a depersonalization, will beget an authority which would be to all people their will and their collective center of consciousness. No person will think for himself. This kind of collectivity was forecast by

Hobbes, by Hegel, and by Marx. Dostoyevsky, looking back on all the states which made themselves absolutes, said that they were only embryos of the new collectivity, which would be destructive:

> Underworld man refuses any organization based on harmony. I shall not be surprised if in the midst of this Universal Reason that is to be there will appear, all of a sudden, and unexpectedly, some common face, or rather cynical and sneering gentleman who with his arms akimbo will say to us: "Now then, you fellows, what about smashing all this reason to bits, sending their logarithms to the devil, and living as we like according to our own silly will." That might not be much, but the annoying thing is that he would immediately get plenty of fellows—men are made like that. And the cause of all this is so that it would scarcely seem worth speaking of: man.

It will be recalled that Dostoyevsky also said: "There are two ages of man—one from the gorilla to the death of God and one from the death of God to the annihilation of man."

It was his constant prediction that a Godless humanity must eventually destroy man. He pictures the Antichrist as a humanitarian and a sociologist who reverses the three temptations of Christ on the Mount and glorifies man without God. This dictator publishes a book on "Peace and Prosperity"; he has seemingly all the compassion of Christ, except that he is evil—or better, he had no scars from suffering for mankind. Cardinal Newman was asked in 1871 who he thought would be the future Goths and Vandals of the next century and he answered: "The lowest class, which is very great in numbers and, unbelieving, will rise up out of the depths of modern cities and be the new scourge of God."

Thomas Aquinas in the thirteenth century said that a socialization and control of personal lives would one day be directed by a "secular city," a *potentia secularis* based on the death of God. The historian Gibbon said that if dominion of mankind fell into the hands of one individual, the world would become a "prison for his adversaries."

Nietzsche taught the Superman who would bring chaos: "I teach you the Superman. Man is something to be surpassed. What have you done to surpass man? All beings hitherto have created something beyond themselves. . . . Would you rather go back to the beast than surpass man? Lo! I teach you the Superman! Let your will say: The Superman *shall be* the meaning of the earth. . . . The self-chosen elect will grow into a chosen people and out of this will grow the Superman. But he must first appear as an atheist—*Thus Spake Zarathustra.*

In the end there will be the "Chaos of the All: which is the exclusion of all purposiveness. "Where are the barbarians of the 20th century? Evidently, they will become consolidated themselves only after enormous socialistic crises." The method by which these barbarians will be created will be by a "transvaluation of values." Evil must be multiplied to a point where there is no remorse. Then the superman can say, "Evil be thou my good; good be thou my evil."

Instruments of Collective Death

The new order introduced by the "Death of God" will be the secular city. The secular city will be the new Bethlehem, and to that new Bethlehem without the Child the Wise Men will bring three gifts: gold, frankincense, and myrrh:

Gold, the symbol of the primacy of profit; the yellow stuff with which one buys pleasure, the status symbol of power in a world where one can buy anything with money.

Frankincense, or the modern science of scent; chemistry and biochemistry which will completely control the genes of man and produce the superman.

Myrrh. It was once used for burial; now it will be the new science of collective death—namely, nuclear weapons.

What more could the secular city ask for than gold which is power over pleasure, frankincense which is power over life, myrrh which is power over death?

The destruction of man will thus be as easy as *A, B, C:* the *A* for Atomic energy; the *B* for Biological transmutations of the human species; and *C* for Chemical nuclear energy.

For this reason, the Vatican Council did not speak of nuclear weapons but of "scientific" weapons, to embrace all three phases of atomic, biological, and chemical warfare.

There is need to mention the importance of gold in the new collectivity, because everyone experiences round about him the love of affluence. But a word might be said about the new frankincense of chemistry and biochemistry in the way of the transmutation of man. One Nobel prize winner in the United States hopes that we can develop through chemistry and biology "a new man with a super brain." Another Nobel prize winner in the United States looks to the day when chemistry can increase brain cells' intensity to the tenth degree. Still another Nobel prize winner suggests enormous deep freezes to keep the sperm cells of men most suited for the human race. Corresponding to this, an English biologist recommends the sterilization of all women by contraceptive hormones, in order to leave fertile only those capable of producing the master race. A French biologist says, "Man is the weakest link in evolution, a blunder in construction, and should be replaced by the superman scientifically engendered." At a conference of Nobel prize winners, W. M. Stanley suggested placing all the embryo plasm of the world in the hands of the chemist; thus the power of the world would be transferred from the nuclear physicist to the chemist. Sir Julian Huxley foresees the day when "electric currents stimulating certain bases of the brain will make all men 'feel happiness.' "

The new myrrh, or the scientific embalmer of collective death, is nuclear warheads. Presently there are sufficient numbers of nuclear weapons in the world to explode over every single person on earth ten tons of nuclear destruction. A few years ago the United States had an overkill of 1,250. This means: Assume the maximum number of enemies in the United States might conceivably have in the future, there is sufficient nuclear energy to kill them over again 1,250 times. At a recent conference of nuclear scientists it was said that, if there was nuclear warfare, the United States would lose in the first thirty minutes between 80 and 125 million people.

Armaments in the world are costing $140 billion a year. The United States and the Soviet Union account for 70 percent of the total. In the United States our expenditure is $63 billion a year. Fifteen other nations are already preparing nuclear energy, for today an atomic bomb has become a status symbol. Nations stockpiling atomic weapons are like misers hiding money under carpets. What is regrettable is that the money spent every year on arms could have raised the per capita income of the underdeveloped countries three times.

Arms and Men

The historical background of nuclear arms shows a progression toward collective death. The first war weapon was a club, used by Cain to shed his brother's blood. This caused him to fall into despair as he became a vagabond on the earth: "Going out from the presence of the Lord," that is, to a God-forsaken life. His descendants built the first city; inasmuch as he had left the Divine Presence, it was the first secular city. Because he was constantly living under anxiety and dread, and because the red thread of another's life had been woven into the fabric of this new civilization, there was constant fear. The first secular city was built in the spirit of cruel egotism, and Cain's red finger marks are on it still.

Among the descendants of Cain was Lamech, the first man to have two wives. One of his sons, Tubalcain, was a smith who worked in brass and iron for service in war. He became the first swordmaker. Lamech, proud of this new war weapon, dedicated a song to his two wives, chanting proudly that if God avenged Cain sevenfold, he and his new sword would not need nor ask the Divine Avenger; he would act himself on the principle: "Vengeance is mine and I will repay, and not merely sevenfold, but seventy and seven times."

His song ran:

"Adah and Zillah, hear my voice,
O wives of Lamech, give ear to my speech:
I have killed a man for wounding me,
A boy was injuring me.

If Cain be avenged seven-fold,
Then Lamech seventy-seven fold."

Setting a naught vengeance which belongs to heaven, he denied judgment and made light of sin's recompense. Such is the thought behind the invention of his sword. He is far ahead of Cain. No longer need he look to God for protection; he can provide more amply for it himself than God did for Cain with a brand on his forehead.

As time went on, weapons became more complicated such as the bow, catapults, and ballistas. The Second Latern Council in 1139 outlawed the crossbow. It was about five or six feet in length, and the arrow discharged was about a yard and a half long, made of metal.

It is sometimes said that Roger Bacon knew of gunpowder in the thirteenth century, but it is more certain that Berthold Schwarz, a German monk of the fourteenth century, also knew of it. In 1892 Maxim invented the silencer, and the press proclaimed, "There will be no more wars, for men will not fight if they cannot hear the explosion of guns." Dynamite, in its modern form, was invented by Nobel. Then journalists wrote: "There will be no more wars, for they will be too destructive. Dynamite is a deterrent." Having made $40 million from his dynamite factories and from explosive nitroglycerin, in an attempt to ease his conscience, he then established the Nobel Prizes for Peace.

Thus the sword of Lamech became longer and longer, more fratricidal, more destructive until at 3:25 P.M. on December 2, 1942, some scientists standing on a squash court gave a signal for a reactor to start working; it began the chain reaction for producing plutonium. The machine worked twenty-eight minutes. This date was the birthday of atomic energy. The scientists opened a bottle of Italian wine and drank, to celebrate the New Age.

Within two months after that birthday, and despite all the secrecy involved, a warning came from another part of the world. At the opening of the session of the Pontifical Academy of Science on February 11, 1943, two years before the bomb dropped in Hiroshima, Pius XII spoke as follows:

Since atoms are extremely small, it is not thought seriously that they might also acquire practical importance. Today, instead, such a question has taken an unexpected form following the results of artificial radio-activity.

It was, in fact, established that in the disintegration which the atom of uranium undergoes when bombarded by neutrons, two or three neutrons are freed, each launching itself—one being able to meet and smash another uranium atom.

From special calculation, it is then ascertained that in such a way in one cubic meter of oxide powder of uranium, in less than one-hundredth of a second, there develops enough energy to elevate a weight of a billion tons sixteen miles into the air—a sum of energy which would substitute for many years the action of all the great power plants of the world.

Above all, it should be of utmost importance that the energy originated by such a machine should not be left to explode—but a means found to control such power with suitable chemical means. Otherwise, there could result not only in a single place but also for our entire universe a dangerous catastrophe.

His second warning was given in 1954.

On the sixteenth day of July, 1945, in an isolated area of mountain-ribbed desert in New Mexico, at 5:30 A.M., a group of nuclear scientists began a countdown beginning at fifty. At zero, an explosion vomited a boiling, surging cloud forty thousand feet into the air, leaving a crater twenty-five feet deep and four hundred feet wide. The secret operation was blasphemously called Trinity.

One of the observers wrote afterward: "It warned us of doomsday and made us feel that we puny things were blasphemous to dare tamper with forces hitherto reserved for the Almighty." President Truman was at the Potsdam conference when his secretary handed him a cable reading, *Babies born.*

On the sixth day of August, 1945, at 9:15 A.M. Japanese time, a plane banked in a sharp turn; a button was pushed, and a mushroom of nuclear destruction rose over Hiroshima. *Babies dead.*

In 1949 Einstein was asked: "What is the future of atomic energy?" He answered: "Come back and see me in *1969.*"

During a dinner conversation in Paris in 1869 recorded in the *Journal* of the Goncourt brothers, Pierre Bethelot predicted that in one hundred years—that is, 1969—"man would know of what the atom was constituted, and would be able, at will, to moderate, extinguish, and light up the sun as if it was a gas lamp."

The Goncourt brothers answered, "We have a feeling that when this time comes to science, God with His white beard will come down to earth, swinging a bunch of keys, and will say to humanity: 'Closing time, gentlemen.' "

It is a coincidence that at that very period when "God is dead," when there is formed the secular city without religion, when Sarte calls "life . . . meaningless and absurd," and Camus writes that "suicide is the only true philosophical problem—is it a coincidence we invented the atomic bomb to blow the earth into meaninglessness?

This is our choice: Collective life through the amortization of humanity or collective death through pride. The moral has been told in the story of two trees growing in a forest. One is a giant tree; the other beneath it is a shriveled tree which engages it in conversation, heaps ridicule upon it not only for climbing so high but also for wasting its strength on roots which cannot be seen. The healthy tree says, "But I grow toward the sun, toward light. And I am dependent on the past for much of my strength."

"There is no sun," says the little shriveled tree. "I cannot see it. Neither can you, and what cannot be verified is void of meaning."

"But I feel the sun. It opens its warmth to me as if it were love; its truth enters into my fibers, and whatever it touches becomes sprouting bud and fruit."

"I feel the warmth of the sun just as much as you do, but this is merely a scientific fact which we cannot verify. It is a condition that is known as spring. It is something that is within us, has no other source than ourselves, and is of our own making. You are wasting your energy and sap with fruit and branches and climbing to the sun and deep roots. I keep all of my sap for my own inner strength.''

And the little shriveled tree continued to grow only in egotism as the days went by, until one day the gardener came and cut it down.

† 20 †

The Sense of Sin

The final condition of the return to the Father's house is a recognition of the sense of sin. After having entered into himself, and after having admitted a need for spiritual pabulum and the freedom which authority alone can purchase, the Prodigal said: "I will go to my Father": "I have sinned against heaven and before thee; I am not worthy to be called thy son; make me as one of thy hired servants. Herein is combined the double element of true redemption, and admission of sin: "I have sinned," and the need of penance, "make me as one of thy hired servants."

Our Blessed Lord never once hints in the parable that, when the young man returned, with a face furrowed with the hard lines of sin, he offered an excuse for his sinfulness. There is no record, there is not even a hint, that he attempted to excuse himself or to extenuate his prodigality. He offered no theory about sin; he did not blame his wicked companions; he did not tell his father that he had inherited a queer complex; he did not say that moral decline is only a myth and that sin is just an illusion; he offered no case to prove that moral lapses are pardonable, not that the great broad world of experience had told him that man was just to sow his wild oats and then forget, live for the future, and have no responsibility toward the past. There were none of these things in the mouth of the Prodigal, and much less was there any such thought in his heart, but only a deep recognition of the horror of sin, and a need of pardon and redemption. "I have sinned against heaven and before thee."

The sense of sin is one of the great and crying needs of the prodigal Western Civilization. It has not yet reached the stage of the Prodigal Son who offered no excuses or extenuation of sin, but it must reach that stage if it is ever to return. The Prodigal did not blame his father, nor his companions, nor his own physical make-up, but Western Civilization is blaming precisely these three things; it places the responsibility for guilt on everything except where it should be placed; namely, in self-will. The Prodigal did not blame his father; but Western Civilization, if it finds sin, does blame the father in the sense that it fixed practically the whole guilt for sin on heredity, which can explain, of course, certain weak tendencies, but cannot wholly explain the guilt. The Prodigal did not blame his evil companions, but Western Civilization does, in the sense that it blames society and environment, which, of course, does play a part in making sin easier but never absolutely constrains the will to give way to it. The Prodigal did not blame his physical self, but Modern Civilization does so, in the sense that it invents very high-sounding names such as the Oedipus complex, introvert, and extrovert, to explain away sin, as if calling a sore throat a streptococcus infection would explain away the sore throat.

It may be interesting to inquire at this point why the modern world has lost its sense of sin. It should be immediately evident that it is the obvious consequence of the loss of the value of man. Under traditional Christianity, a man was a theological creature, an adopted son of God and a member of the Mystical Body of Christ; in the eighteenth and nineteenth centuries man became a philosophical thing bound to God by some vague ties of creaturehood. But man today is only a biological phenomenon with no other destiny than that of the worm he crushes under his heel. Once one loses hold on the primary dogma that man has a moral end, and that his actions, thoughts, and words in this life are all registered in the Book of Life, and therefore will one day determine his eternal destiny, sin becomes meaningless. The modern mind has forgotten the dogma of man, and hence cannot avoid forgetting the morals of man, for one is the corollary of the other. Deny that God is interested in the behavior of men and you immediately create a society in which man is uninterested in the behavior of his fellow man.

The great mistake of the nineteenth century was to believe that the intellectual basis of Christian doctrine about God and man, and their mutual relations, could be abolished without in any way impairing morals. Dogmas were considered impossible, but ethics were indispensable; doctrine was ridiculous but morals sublime; the Cross was folly, but the Sermon on the Mount was a masterpiece. Practically all advanced Victorian minds proceeded on the assumption that you could obliterate the religious beliefs of a nation without affecting its moral standards. It may take a generation or two to prove the fallacy of the statement: "It makes no difference what you believe; what matters is how you live"; but the world sooner or later discovers that it does make a difference, for we act on our beliefs, and if we think wrongly, we act wrongly. If we do not suit our lives to dogmas, we will end by suiting dogmas to our lives.

Minds no longer object to the Church, because of the way they *think,* but because of the way they *live.* They no longer have difficulty with the Creed, but with her Commandments; they remain outside her saving waters, not because they cannot accept the doctrine of Three Persons in One God, but because they cannot accept the moral of two persons in one flesh; not because Infallibility is too complex, but because the veto on Birth Control is too hard; not because the Eucharist is too sublime, but because Penance is too exacting. Briefly, the heresy of our day is not the heresy of thought; it is the heresy of action.

We are living in a time when the old forms of sensationalism of a generation ago are now regarded as banal; words such as "obedience," "honor," and "purity," which once stood for the desirable and the sacred, now stand either for weakness, or restraint of liberty. Everything that is good, everything that is just, everything that is noble in our civilization is a reflection of abiding Christian principles. But they are fading away; the borderland between light and darkness is growing dimmer, and we are about to pass over into the hinterland of darkness and ruin. As a matter of fact, there has been a greater de-Christianization of society in the past hundred years than in any other given period of Christian history. As an evidence of how much God and morality have passed out of contemporary civilization, contrast two works, one written in the beginning of the fifth century, the other in the beginning of the nineteenth; namely, *The City of God* of St. Augustine and the *Philosophy of History* of Frederick Schlegel. The first is manifestly more spiritual, but there is common to both, an admission that the purposes of God work themselves out in history, and that civilization is unintelligible without the Lord of the Universe.

Now contrast two works written in the past hundred years, almost to the exact year. *The Philosophy of History* of Schlegel which was just mentioned, and the *Outline of History* by H. G. Wells. The Providence of God mattered in the first, but it is not even mentioned in the second. Today there is a general atrophy of a vital conviction that there is a righteous purpose sovereign in history. Men today model their lives solely in relation to economic interest rather than the common good and the glory of God.

There is probably no greater proof of the decline of the idea of sin than the widespread popularity of Marxism. There is some similarity between Rousseau and Marx in the sense that both thought man naturally good in the theological sense of the term. Rousseau said man was born good but society ruined him; Marx said man was born good, but capitalism ruined him. Society and capitalism both take the place of original sin. Rousseau "redeemed" man by the "Social Contract," and Marx by the "Classless Class" or the proletarian revolution.

The proletariat became the new elect for Marx very much as the bourgeoisie became the elect for Calvin, with this difference. Election for Calvin was by the predestination of God; election for Marx is by materialism. All the modern solutions since the days of Rousseau have gone wrong by forgetting man is a fallen creature. Marx thinks that by eliminating Capitalism, he established original justice. It is sheer illusion to think that the new order will eliminate social injustices and restore the peace of the original Paradise. Man has sinned and he will sin again, and Communism is no redemption for sin; it is only forced tranquillity.

What adds to the seriousness of this view is that the world's fallen state is accompanied, not by an increased, but by a decreased sense of sin. The world sins more, but is less mindful of its seriousness. Paganism sinned, too, but the sin of modern paganism has the added seriousness of having betrayed an ideal which the older pagans had not; namely, the ideal of Christ.

By this I do mean to say that when the world accepted the faith and morals of the Church, that the world was free of sinners. As a matter of fact there were men just as wicked in the thirteenth century as there are in the twentieth; there were souls just as immoral in the second century as there are today. But there is this great difference between the sinners of a Christianized civilization and the sinners of our day: the sinners of the Christian civilization *knew they were sinners;* the sinners of modern civilization think they are saints; the sinners of the Christian civilization broke the law, but admitted the law *was right;* the sinners of modern civilization break the law, and say that the law is wrong. The sinners of Christian ages knew they were wrong, and wished they were right. The sinners of our day, on the contrary, do wrong, but do not want to be right. As we have already seen, there is hope for any civilization which breaks a law but never calls in question the truth of the law; but there is no hope for a civilization that breaks a law and then denies it.

Man is powerless to resist evil if he does not recognize it as such, and deceives himself when he becomes indifferent to evil; his whole personality immediately begins to dissolve, for the power of conscience is inseparably bound up with the denunciation of evil. And this is precisely what our world is doing today; the very beliefs on which the best culture of the world was built are now called in question. Even the distinction between good and evil is lost, and now only a sense of civic loyalty remains. The Prophet Isaias sounded such a decadence in his day: "Woe to you that call evil good, and good evil; that put darkness for light, and light for darkness; that put bitter for sweet and sweet for bitter."

If we called sin by its right name it would lose all of its seductiveness. Hell can be made attractive, only by surfacing it with the gold of Paradise. It is unfortunate indeed that those who think unspeakable filth have the gift of writing good English. Their readers feel they are justified in reading the book because the style is good. We might just as well say that it is permissible to take poison provided it is sugar coated.

Now this loss of the sense of sin is serious. Civilization begins to go to pieces when it loses its respect and love for saints and begins to interest itself in the lives of criminals. Lecky, in his *History of European Morals,* writes in a very eloquent passage that, "While the Greek and Roman world was perplexed by the mystery of being, and shadowed by the suffering of life, and while it was moved by the examples of great heroism, there was no sense of sin possessing men's hearts. Remorse was an unknown passion, and penitent shame was impossible. The burden of guilt did not rest on even a criminal's heart. Men looked on deeds of infamy and were not shocked. The sin of the world and its moral corruption infected the air. Men were naked and not ashamed, not because they were innocent, but because no sense of guilt assailed them."

Just how far the world has departed from the standard of the Cross one need hardly ask. How seldom does one find anyone outside the Father's house doing penance for his sins, i.e., applying the Cross of Christ to his soul? How often does a writer of immoral books, when he comes to a consciousness of the souls he has polluted, end his days in prayer and reparation? How often does a man who has gained great wealth unjustly, ever think of setting his soul right with God?

Rarely indeed is it recorded in the twentieth century of a sinner seeking to enter the kingdom of God by doing penance. It is rare, because the modern ideal has changed. The absolute ideal no longer is goodness, but success. The poor man may be good, but to the modern mind he has failed if he is unsuccessful. Such an ideal renders penance and the desire of redemption impossible. The modern man is grateful so long as he does not die poor, for to him "what doth it profit a man if he save his soul and lose the whole world?" His deathbed is one of unctuous self-esteem and self-complacency, but never a cry for the mercy and love of God.

It is no wonder that Communism has decided to make a clean sweep of what it calls "bourgeois morality," which is really only a flimsy sentimentalism expressed by catchwords such as "leave the world better than you find it." Communism must be given the credit of seeing the fallacy of morals divorced from a dogmatic basis, and that basis it has tried to supply. For Communism an act is good if it subserves the economic prosperity of the State. The final end in such a system of morality is the political collective. The test of any act is the good of the State.

But even this moral code is just as unsatisfactory as the "higher-living" ideal of the "bourgeois moralists." The question they have to answer is this: What is the final good of the proletariat State? Why slave and work? Why permit personality and freedom for cultural and religious pursuits to be strangled for the good of the State? What will eventually happen to the State? According to the second law of thermodynamics, the State is one day destined to perish, and with it all the little human cogwheels that made its big flywheel spin. But if the State is destined to die, then the final end of a good and bad action are the same; namely, death and dissolution. If the waves of the seas are to wash away the sandcastles built on the shore, what difference does it make if I build them six feet tall or six inches tall? If all our actions are to be cursed with a gigantic futility, why do good rather than evil; why work for the economic good of the State which will perish, rather than my own economic good which will also fade into dust?

Communism cracks at that one point: What is the use of economically dominating the earth if we cannot take it with us? The death of man renders all our Titanism and worldly conquest mean and negligible. A funeral for that reason is the expression of the futility of the Communistic State for in the presence of every corpse, men will ask themselves: "What doth it profit to gain the whole world?" Joseph Roth in his book *Anti-Christ* pictures Death speaking to the body of Lenin, whose corpse the Communists conquered even though they could not conquer death. That corpse, the author says is "like an ostentatious, but, of course, at the same time childish threat to Death, who is shown that his victim can none the less be preserved—like jewelry which is no longer worn." Death speaks and says: "Your threat is childish and your pride is folly. It is my task to take from this earth not his countenance but that which was his life and which you love; namely, his breath. He is extinguished, like a lamp. I have taken wick and oil, and you may keep the vessel, with which I am not concerned. It was his flame which you loved, and his light! Why are you now flaunting the insignificant vessel in which they were contained? Many great lights have I already extinguished, and monuments were erected to them. That is wiser than what you are doing! For a monument does not deny, but confirms the law according to which I act. And when it confirms me, it also conquers me. A monument, however cheap, is the sign that the living remember the dead, and it is an impotent but reverent form of resurrection. You, however, do not cause the dead man to be resurrected. You give permanence to his corpse and refuse to let it molder. Why should a corpse not fall into dust and ashes? Did man come from paraffin and wax, to become once more paraffin and wax? If you have as much respect for the dead man as you say you have, do you not comprehend that he should not be exhibited as a barber exhibits his wigs or wax busts. Why do you flaunt your achievement in my face—in the face of Death? You have withheld nothing from me, but you have detracted from your own dignity—your own, and that of your dead."

The most terrible consequence of the loss of the sense of sin, as was hinted above, is that it destroys the yearning for redemption, for a man who does not know cancer is devouring him, feels no need of a physician. During the last century the theory of evolution, applied to sociology, resulted in the false idea of "progress" which led men to believe that cosmic laws guaranteed his necessary and inevitable perfection. In those days of progress, man had faith in tomorrow, faith in big business, faith in science, faith in utilitarian education, faith in common sense, faith in faith. When "progress" cracked, all the baseless duties of unreasonable faith collapsed, and we found ourselves not evolving but dissolving. The notion of the "inevitable" then substituted itself for "progress." Having lost the purposiveness of human life in relation to the beatific vision, faith gave way to despair. Now men feel they are caught in the web of circumstances and that decay must eventually work itself out before things become better.

This is where the doctrine of Redemption asserts itself, as the antithesis of despair. It provides in the final place, an explanation for the failure of the law of progress, by giving an explanation of the otherwise unaccountable fact, that what the good men will to do, that, they do not; and the evil which they will not, that, they do.[1] Secondly, it provides an escape from the "inevitable," by assuring us that the most important thing about sin is not its sinfulness, but the fact that it can be atoned. Man need not slide down to ruin; he need not be the plaything of circumstances; he can be remade, reshaped, and redeemed for nobler ends, for within history there is a Redeemer.

[1] Here the Catholic point of view stresses the order of sin, and the order of grace. Too often they both are overlooked. A solution to our social evils must recognize both. Man in his fallen or natural state is prone to evil, but raised to the supernatural state of grace, he can hope for strength to overcome himself. In Adam we are subject to our nature; in Christ we are masters of our senses. Ovid: "I see the better things of life; I follow the wicked." As noted, man is a member of the society of Adam and the society of Christ. The human race as a society has a natural head in Adam and its spiritual head in Christ. The members joined to the head constitute the body (*De Malo*, q. 4, art. 1). Therefore, there are two bodies, one after the flesh, the other after the spirit. When the head of the former body, Adam, sinned, original sin passed on to us, not as a personal sin, but as a sin of nature; when Christ paid the price of redemption, His graces came to us. If no Adam, there would be no human race; if no Christ, there would be no regenerated humanity. With this understanding, our conclusion is that the members of Christ's body can speak of victory, when they build the City of God and not the City of Man. However, the primal curse of humanity cannot be ignored. Pope Leo XIII (*Rerum Novarum*) points out that "to suffer and endure is the lot of humanity. . . . If there are any who pretend differently . . . they delude the people. . . . Nothing is more useful than to look upon the world as it really is and at the same time to look elsewhere for a solace for its troubles."

See Sheen, F. J., *The Mystical Body*, note 1, 35; also notes 2 and 3, 36.

Leo XIII in his Encyclical *Exeunte Jam Anno*, gives due treatment to original sin and its consequences as affecting the ordering of Christian life.

Redemption is not an exclusively individual affair between God and the soul; it does not merely entail faithfulness to the ethical teachings of our Lord, not constitute only a challenge to overcome our individual difficulties. Redemption is something social as well as personal, for man is a member of society. To proclaim its social character, He who came unto His own and was rejected, set up His Cross, not in the individual heart, but in the world; it was placarded before the eyes of men, in the open air, under the noonday sun, at the very crossroads of civilization, to remind us all that our destiny is the kingdom of God.

That Cross was so social it began a new world; it gave men new standards of living, a new way of measuring and judging the sorrows and trials of this life; it offered a different balance in which to weigh the earth against their souls. It gave men a fresh start, even though it was a late start, another hope, a safer orientation, a brighter vision, and it did all this, because it was so very revolutionary. It upset worldly standards as the Lord one day upset the tables of the money-changers in the Temple; it made the first last, and the last first; exalted the humble, and humbled the exalted; made enemies loves and blessed persecutors; forgave the sinners and put a premium on losing a life in order to save it. Looking down the corridors of time it made all subsequent revolutions but trivial upstarts, for they failed to affect the soul of society; even the Communistic revolution was incomplete for it still leaves hate and does not say, "forgive"; it still leaves earthliness and does not say: "This day thou shalt be with Me in Paradise"; it still leaves despair, and does not say: "Father, into Thy hands I commend My spirit."

Now this redemptive love of the cross did not stop with the Good Friday of nineteen hundred years ago; as long as sin remains the Cross still stands. Until the last sheaf is garnered into the everlasting barns, the Reaper of souls remains in the field. The souls, such as that of the penitent thief, won on that first day of the cross, and the souls won ever since by grace issuing from the cross, constitute the kingdom of God, or the Mystical Body of Christ. The members of this society did not create the kingdom of God; the kingdom of God in Christ the First Born pre-existed them. The condition of incorporation with the Mystical Body of Christ is the acceptance of the Cross and all that it means: "If any man will come after Me, let him deny himself, and take up his cross and follow Me." "They that are Christ's have crucified their flesh with its vices and concupiscences." This corporation of the lovers of the cross under the inspiration of the Crucified, institutes the new society through which Christ redeems the world. It is the new humanity, the spiritual corporation, in which each individual draws his strength directly from Christ Himself through the Mass which is Calvary re-enacted and through the Sacraments which are Calvary distributed.

This Mystical Body of Christ which accepts the revolutionary standard of the Cross, is the leaven in the mass of the world, revealing to each man the true end of life: it is to the new world what Judaism was to the Gentiles, what the soul is to the body, what light is to darkness—the channel of social regeneration. It does not make everyone in the world saintly, for man is still free; it does not make everyone a lover of the Cross, for many are still selfish; it does not relieve the world of suffering, for its kingdom of happiness is not in this world; it has not saved modern civilization, because modern civilization has not tried it, but only its substitute, and imitations. However, it does secure a recognition of a supernatural criterion and a normal pattern of life, which, if accepted, would enable the mass of men to fulfill their destiny on earth without being obliged to impossible heroism; it does provide an eternal end rather than a temporal end, as the basis of social action, and that means everything; it does make life reasonable by assuring man that he lives in a world of good and evil opportunity, where his choice must be a matter of significance for himself and his fellow men; it does influence the economic order by condemning the idiocy of burning wheat in a land of hunger, and of calling men "superfluous" in a universe where every man has an immortal soul; and a suppressing man for the sake of the State when a man is a citizen of the kingdom of God, as well as the kingdom of Caesar.

The social character of the Redemption is based on the principle that "the same Christ is assuredly the source of the individual's salvation; neither is there a salvation in any other, for there is no other name under heaven, given to men whereby we may be saved." He is the author of prosperity and of genuine happiness for every citizen and for the nation. The happiness of the State comes from exactly the same source as the happiness of the individual, the State being nothing else than a number of individuals living in harmony. The faithful, moreover, by diligently meditating on these matters will gain much strength and courage enabling them to fashion their own lives on the true Christian ideal. For if to Christ our Lord is given all power in heaven and on earth; and if this power that Christ wields is exercised over human nature in its entirety, it is abundantly clear that not one of our faculties is exempt from His all-embracing sovereign sway. "He must reign in the mind of man, which ought to assent with perfect submission and firm, unwavering belief to the revealed truths and doctrines of Christ. He must reign in man's will, which ought to obey the laws and precepts of God. He must reign in the heart of man, which ought to reject the cravings of nature and love God above all things and cleave to Him alone. He must reign in the body and in its members, which ought to serve as instruments towards the interior sanctification of our souls, or as the Apostle Paul says, of instruments of justice unto God." (Encyclical of Pius XI on the *Kingship of Christ*.) The redemptive society of the Mystical Body of Christ is not a movement of social reform; it is not a sentimental loyalty toward which men may turn after all human remedies have failed; rather it is the regeneration of society through the spiritual rebirth of the men and women who compose it. Social order is not organized from the outside but vivified from the inside by giving human life a meaning and a spiritual significance. Political alliances, economic plans promise quicker results but they are bound to fail so long as society pins its faith in material ends, and appeals only to utilitarian sanctions. The meaning and spiritual significance of society can be supplied only by the Cross. Human society may continue to offer men the *means* of existence, but the Church with its Cross alone can offer the *object* of existence which determines the morality of the means. Man has indeed missed the mark, but there is a mark; and that mark is to be attained not through a higher will, but through a new level of being and a new energy brought to man through the Person of Christ, and made available through His social existence in His Church.

It may take the modern world a long time before it is willing to cry out with the Prodigal: "I have sinned," but until that day arrives it can expect no healing ointment for its broken wings. There is no redemption except from sin; there is no hope for betterment until there has been an admission of failure. Our social structure, then, must one day admit the fallacy of "business is business"; it must judge its economic policies not by their feasibility but by their morality; and it must confess that economics and politics are but branches of moral theology and philosophy, i.e., they can be sinful if they violate the ultimate end of man. The moral necessity of man's attaining the full perfection of his personality circumscribes human action in the domestic, political, economic, and religious spheres. Every act is a moral act, even a religious act; nothing is excluded whether it be selling of a can of milk, or the formation of a great corporation. Hence economic policy can save a man's soul as well as damn it. Morality is involved in the realities of industries, finances, and government, and the assumption that these things are governed by non-ethical forces is false. Business can crucify Christ just as well as pride, and therefore it has just as much need of redemption.

The ignoring of the moral basis of the economic order, and therefore the denial of sin, has been the conspicuous attitude of the social order for many decades, during which time society has ignored the Christian pattern of life. In that time the elements of collapse have gathered on all sides: the loss of human purpose, the dissatisfaction of the masses, the glorification of the economic end, the loosening of the moral bonds and the gradual dehumanization of men in the great collective. And what is to be done about it? What would we do if we found a live salmon on top of the Empire State Building? We would try to restore it as quickly as possible to its environment. And that is the only thing to be done with the world. Put it back in its environment of religion and morality. And all the discussion about politics and economics divorced from the moral order is just as stupid as to legislate for salmon on skyscrapers. It is a change of heart, of mind, of soul, and not exclusively a new economics which is needed; and this new heart can be found only at the foot of the Cross where things are measured according to their true worth. Once men see that Cross elevated before their eyes at the elevation of the host, they begin to realize that three score and ten years of life is a time for testing—a moment taken out of eternal life in which to say "yes" or "nay" to Divine Love. We have been living for some time on the margin of Christianity, but now the Cross is beginning to fade from the eyes of men. The result is we are face to face with disturbances from which the earlier generations were saved. We must now choose between having society radically rearranged by the forces of sin which crucify, or spiritually regenerated by the Cross which redeems.

At the present moment, whether we admit it or not, there is only one Power which stands between the modern world and absolute chaos and decay, and that is the Power of Christ in the Mass with His arms and ours outstretched to the Heavenly Father making intercession for the world. Suspended between heaven and earth, He reconciles the two by something which is not wholly of either, and yet of both. That Power alone is left to declare unto the world that the life of man is fraught with wonderful and holy purposes, and that even though sin doth abound, saving grace and redemption may yet more abound. There is no escaping the Cross, for the simple reason that there is no goal gained without the effort, and no victory won without the battle. To keep whispering to ourselves sweet but false consolations, to look for the end when we are only at the beginning, to go round the Cross instead of climbing on, these are but the materials out of which a cross is made—and a cross where one bar is at variance and contradiction with another, the most insoluble mystery of all.

But we must enter into that higher plane of making earth a steppingstone to heaven, where nobility stands the test, where love spells sacrifice, where the horizontal bar of death meets the vertical bar of life in the Person of Christ on the Cross reconciling both. This is the Crucifix wherein we confess not the mysterious ways of Job, but enter into them for our eternal joy and consolation. Once united with the Crucified as we are in the Mass, we begin to understand, that everywhere else, others promise us sin excused, sin discounted, sin denied, sin explained away, but only at the foot of the Cross do we ever experience the beautiful Divine contradiction of sin forgiven.

✝ 21 ✝

Our Final Choice

There comes a time in the life of every man when at the supreme and tragic hour of death his friends and relative ask, "How much did he leave?" It is just at that split second God is asking, "How much did he take with him?" It is only the latter question that matters, for it is only our works that follow us. The story of life is brief: "It is appointed unto men once to die and after this the judgment," for "the Son of Man shall come in the glory of His Father with His angels, and then will He render to every man according to his works." In the general forgetfulness of the Christian religion, which has passed over our civilization like a foul miasma, this great truth that a judgment follows death has been ignored in the moral outlook of the universe. Our souls can profit much from meditation upon it and its two important features; namely, its necessity and its nature.

All nature testifies to the necessity of judgment. Everywhere below man nature reveals itself as passing sentence on those who refuse to obey her laws. We need only look around us in the hospitals, prisons, and asylums to see that nature, like a judge seated in judgment, is squaring her accounts with those who violate her laws. If the body has abused itself by excess, nature takes revenge and passes the judgment of disease and infirmity. If a fragment of a star breaks from its central core and swings out of its orbit, nature passes the judgment that it shall burn itself out in space.

Nature settles her account with natural things here and now. But the moral side of the universe has not made its lasting reckoning with every man on this side of the grave: there is too much anguished innocence, too much unpunished wrong; too much suffering of the good; too much prosperity of the evil; too much pain for those who obey God's laws; too much pleasure for those who disobey them; too much good repute for those who sin unseen; too much scorn for those who pray unseen; too many unsung saints; too many glorified sinners; too many Pilates who act as righteous judges; too many Christs who go down to crucifixion; too many proud and vain souls who say, "I have sinned and nothing has happened."

But the reckoning day must come, and just as once a year each business man must balance his accounts, so too that important hour must come when every soul must balance its accounts before God. For life is like a cash register, in that every account, every thought, every deed, like every sale, is registered and recorded. And when the business of life is finally done, then God pulls from out the registry of our souls that slip of our memory on which is recorded our merits and demerits, our virtues and our vices—the basis of the judgment on which shall be decided eternal life or eternal death. We may falsify our accounts until that day of judgment, for God permits the wheat and the cockle to grow unto the harvest, but then, "in the time of the harvest, I will say to the reaper: gather up first the cockle and bind it into bundles to burn, but the wheat gather ye into my barn."

But what is the nature of judgment? In answer to this question we are more concerned with the particular judgment at the moment of death, than with the general judgment when all nations of the earth stand before their God. Judgment is a recognition both on the part of God and on the part of the soul.

First of all, it is a recognition on the part of God. Imagine two souls appearing before the sight of God, one in the state of grace, the other in the state of sin. Grace is a participation in the nature and life of God. Just as a man participates in the nature and life of his parents by being born of his parents, so too a man who is born of the Spirit of God by Baptism participates in the nature of God— the life of God, as it were, flows through his veins, impringing an unseen but genuine likeness. When, therefore, God looks upon a soul in the state of grace, He sees in it a likeness of His own nature. Just as a father recognizes his own son because of likeness of nature, so too Christ recognizes the soul in the state of grace in virtue of resemblance to Him, and says to the soul: "Come ye blessed of My Father: I am the natural Son, you are the adopted son. Come into the Kingdom prepared for you from all eternity."

God looks into the other soul that is in the state of sin and has not that likeness, and just as a father knows his neighbor's son is not his own, so too God, looking at the sinful soul and failing to see therein the likeness of His own flesh and blood, does not recognize it as His own kind, and says to it as He said in the parable of the bridegroom "I know you not"—and it is a terrible thing not to be known by God.

Not only is sin a recognition from God's point of view, but it is also a recognition from man's point of view. Just suppose that while cleaning your car, or your house, a very distinguished person was announced at the door. You would probably act differently than if you were thoroughly clean, well dressed, and presentable. In such an unclean condition you would ask to be excused, saying you were not fit to appear in the sight of such a person. When a soul is before the sight of God, it acts in much the same manner. Standing before the tremendous majestic presence of almighty God, it does not plead, it does not argue, it does not entreat, it does not demand a second hearing, it does not protest the judgment, for it sees itself as it really is. In a certain sense, it judges itself, God merely sealing the judgment. If it sees itself clean and alive with the life of God, it runs to the embrace of love, which is heaven, just as a bird released from its cage soars into the skies. If it sees itself slightly stained and the robes of its Baptism remediably soiled. it protests that it is not to enter into the sight of purity, and hence throws itself into the purifying flames of purgatory. If it sees itself irremediably vitiated, having no likeness whatever to the purity and holiness of God; if it has lost all affection for the things of spirit, then it could no more endure the presence of God than a man who abhors beauty could endure the pleasure of music, art, and poetry. Why, heaven would be hell to such a soul, for it would be as much out of place in the holiness of heaven as a fish out of water. Hence, recognizing its own ungodliness, its own distaste for the purity of God, it casts itself into hell in the same way that a stone, released from the hand, falls to the ground. Only three states, therefore, are possible after the particular judgment: heaven, purgatory, and hell. Heaven is love without pain, purgatory is pain with love; and hell is pain without love.

Time is the one thing that makes real pleasure impossible, for the simple reason that it does not permit us to make a club sandwich of pleasures. By its very nature it forbids us to have many pleasures together under the penalty of having none of them at all. By the mere fact that I exist in time, it is impossible for me to combine the pleasures of marching with the old guard of Napoleon, and at the same time, advancing under the flying eagles of Caesar. By the mere fact that I live in time, I cannot enjoy simultaneously the winter sports of the Alps, and the limpid waters of the Riviera. Time makes it impossible for me to be stirred by the oratory of a Demosthenes, and at the same time to listen to the melodious accents of the great Bossuet. Time does not permit me to combine the prudence that comes with age and the buoyancy that belongs to youth. It is the one thing which prevents me from gathering around the same festive table with Aristotle, Socrates, Thomas Aquinas, and Mercier in order to learn the secrets of great minds in solving the riddles of a universe. If it were not for time, Dante and Shakespeare could have sipped tea together, and Homer even now might tell us his stories in English. It is all very nice and lovely to enjoy the mechanical perfections of this age of luxury, but there are moments when I would like to enjoy the calm and peace of the Middle Ages, but time will not permit it. If I live in the twentieth century, I must sacrifice the pleasures of the thirteenth, and if I enjoy the Athenian age of Pericles, I must be denied the Florentine age of Dante.

Thus it is that time makes it impossible to combine pleasures. I know there are advertisements which would invite us to dine and dance, but no one can do both comfortably at one and the same time. All things are good, and yet none can be enjoyed except in their season, and the enjoyment must always be tinged with the regret that time will demand their surrender. Time gives me things, but it also takes them away. When it does give, it gives but singly, and thus life becomes but "just one fool thing after another."

This thought suggests the suspicion that if time makes the combination of pleasures impossible, then if I could ever transcend time, I might, in some way, increase my happiness, and this I find to be true, for every conscious desire to prolong a pleasure is a desire to make it an enduring "now." Like cats before the fire, we want to prolong the pleasure indefinitely; we want it to be permanent and not successive.

Go back in the storehouse of your memory, and you will find ample proof that it is always in those moments when you are least conscious of the passing of time that you most thoroughly enjoy the pleasures of time. How often it happens, for example, when listening to an absorbing conversation or the thrilling experiences of a much traveled man, that the hours pass by so quickly we are hardly conscious of them, and we say, "The time passes like everything." What is true of a delightful conversation is also true of esthetic pleasures. I dare say that very few would ever notice the passing of time listening to an orchestra translate the beauty of one of Beethoven's works. In just the proportion that it pleases and thrills, it makes us unconscious of how long we were absorbed by its melodies. The contrary fact illustrates the same truth. The more we notice time, the less we are being interested. If our friends keep looking at their watches while we till a story, we can be very sure that they are being bored by our story. A man who keeps his eye on the clock is not the man who is interested in his work. The more we notice the passing of time, the less is our pleasure, and the less we notice the passing of time, the greater is our pleasure.

These psychological facts of experience testify that not only is time the obstacle of enjoyment, but escape from it is the essential of happiness. Suppose we could enlarge upon our experience in such a way as to imagine ourselves completely outside of time and succession, in a world where there would never be a "before" nor an "after," but only a "now." Suppose we could go out to another existence where the great pleasures of history would not be denied us because of their historical incompatibility, but all unified in a beautiful hierarchial order, like a pyramid in that all would minister to the very unity of our personality. Suppose I say that I could reach a point of timelessness at which all the enjoyments and beauties and happiness of time could be reduced to those three fundamental unities which constitute the perfection of our being, namely, life, and truth, and love, for into these three all pleasures can be resolved.

Suppose first of all that I could reduce to a single focal point all the pleasures of life, so that in the now which never looked before nor after, I could enjoy the life that seems to be in the sea when its restless bosom is dimpled with calm, as well as the urge of life that seems to be in all the hill-encircling brooks that loiter to the sea; the life which provokes the dumb, dead sod to tell its thoughts in violets; the life which pulsates through a springtime blossom as the swinging cradle for the fruit; the life of the flowers as they open the chalice of their perfume to the sun; the life of the birds as the great heralds of song and messengers of joy; the life of all the children that run shouting to their mother's arms; the life of all the parents that beget a life like unto their own; and the life of the mind that on the wings of an invisible thought strikes out to the hid battlements of eternity to the life whence all living comes. . . .

Suppose that in addition to concentrating all the life of the universe in a single point, I could also concentrate in another focal point all the truths of the world, so that I could know the truth the astronomer seeks as he looks up through his telescope, and the truth the biologist seeks as he looks down through his miscroscope; the truth about the heavens, and who shut up the sea with doors when it did burst forth as issuing from a womb; the truth about the hiding place of darkness and the treasure house of hail, and the cave of the winds, the truth about the common things: why fire, like a spirit, mounts to the

heavens heavenly, and why gold, like clay, falls to the earth
earthly; the truth the philosopher seeks as he tears apart with
his mind the very wheels of the universe; the truth the theologian seeks as he used Revelation to unravel the secrets of God
which far surpass those that John heard as he leaned his head
upon the breast of his Master. . . .

Suppose that over and above all these pleasures of life and
truth, there could be unified in another focal point all the de-
lights and beauties of love that have contributed to the happiness of the universe: the love of the patriot for his country; the
love of the soldier for his cause; the love of the scientist for his
discovery; the love of the flowers as they smile upon the sun;
the love of the earth at whose breast all creation drinks the milk
of life; the love of mothers, who swing open the great portals of
life that a child may see the light of day; the love of friend for
friend to whom he could reveal his heart through words; the
love of spouse for spouse; the love of husband for wife; and
even the love of angel for angel, and the angel for God with a
fire and heat sufficient to enkindle the hearts of ten thousand
times ten thousand worlds. . . .

Suppose that all the pleasures of the world could be brought
to these three focal points of life and truth and love, just as the
rays of the sun are brought to unity in the sun; suppose that all
the successive pleasures of time could be enjoyed at one and
the same now; and suppose that these points of unity on which
our hearts and minds and souls would be directed, would not
merely be three abstractions, but that the focal point in which
all the pleasures of life were concentrated would be a life personal enough to be a Father, and that the focal point of truth in
which all the pleasures of truth were concentrated, would not
merely be an abstract truth, but a truth personal enough to be a
Word or a Son, and that that focal point of love in which all the
pleasures of love were concentrated, would be not merely an
abstract love, but a love personal enough to be a Holy Spirit;
and suppose that once elevated to that supreme height, happiness would be so freed from limitations that it would include
these three as one, not in succession, but with a permanence;
not as in time, but as in the timeless—then we would have
eternity, then we would have God! The Father, Son, and Holy

Ghost: Perfect Life, Perfect Truth, Perfect Love. Then we would have happiness—and that would be heaven.

Will the pleasures of that timelessness with God and that enjoyment of life and truth and love which is the Trinity be in any way comparable to the pleasures of time? Is there anyone on this earth that will tell me about heaven? Certainly there are three faculties to which one might appeal, namely, to what one has seen, to what one has heard, and to what one can imagine. Will heaven surpass all the pleasures of the eye, and the ear, and the imagination? First of all, will it be as beautiful as some of the things that can be seen? I have seen the Villa d'Este of Rome with its long lanes of ilex and laurel, and its great avenues of cypress trees, all full of what might be called the vivacity of quiet and living silence; I have seen a sunset on the Mediterranean when two clouds came down like pillars to form a brilliant red tabernacle for the sun and it glowing like a golden host; I have seen, from the harbor, the towers and the minarets of Constantinople pierce through the mist which hung over them like a silken veil; I have seen the chateau country of France and her Gothic cathedrals aspiring heavenward like prayers; I have seen the beauties of the castles of the Rhine, and the combination of all these visions almost makes me think of the doorkeeper of the Temple of Diana who used to cry out to those who entered: "Take heed to your eye," and so I wonder if the things of eternity will be as beautiful as the combined beauty of all the things which I have seen. . . .

I have not seen all the beauties of nature, others I have heard of that I have not seen: I have heard of the beauties of the hanging gardens of Babylon, of the pomp and dignity of the palaces of Doges, of the brilliance and glitter of the Roman Forum as its foundations rocked with the tramp of Rome's resistless legions; I have heard of the splendor of the Temple of Jerusalem as it shone like a jewel in the morning sun; I have heard of the beauties of the garden of Paradise where four-fold river flowed through lands rich with gold and onyx, a garden made beautiful as only God knows how to make a beautiful garden; I have heard of countless other beauties and joys of nature which tongue cannot describe, nor touch of brush convey, and I wonder if all the joys and pleasures of heaven will be as great as the combined beauty of all the things of which I heard. . . .

Beyond what I have heard and seen, there are things which I can imagine: I can imagine a world in which there never would be pain, nor disease, nor death; I can imagine a world wherein every man would live in a castle, and in that commonwealth of castles there would be a due order of justice without complaint or anxiety; I can imagine a world in which the winter would never come, and in which the flowers would never fade, and the sun would never set; I can imagine a world in which there would always be a peace and a quiet without idleness, a profound knowledge of things without research, a constant enjoyment without satiety; I can imagine a world which would eliminate all the evils and diseases and worries of life, and combine all of its best joys and happiness, and I wonder if all the happiness of heaven would be like the happiness of earth which I can imagine. . . .

Will eternity be anything like what I have seen, or what I have heard, or what I can imagine? No, eternity will be nothing like anything I have seen, heard or imagined. Listen to the voice of God: "Eye hath not seen, nor ear heard, neither hath it entered into the heart of man what things God hath prepared for them that love Him."

If the timeless so much surpasses time that there can be found no parallel for it, then I begin to understand the great mystery of the shape of the human heart. The human heart is not shaped like a Valentine heart, perfect and regular in contour; it is slightly irregular in shape as if a small piece of it were missing out of its side. That missing part may very well symbolize a piece that a spear tore out of the universal heart of humanity on the Cross, but it probably symbolizes something more. It may very well mean that when God created each human heart, He kept a small sample of it in heaven, and sent the rest of it into the world of time where it would each day learn the lesson that it could never be really happy, never be really wholly in love, and never be really *whole* hearted until it went back again to the timeless to recover the sample which God had kept for it for all eternity.

Copyright Acknowledgements